BUT WHERE SHALL WISDOM BE FOUND?

ABERDEEN UNIVERSITY PRESS

British Library Cataloguing in Publication Data.
A catalogue record for this book is available from the
British Library.

Department of Divinity with Religious Studies
King's College, University of Aberdeen
AB9 2UB

First published in Great Britain by
Aberdeen University Press

Printed and bound by Astra Print and Design, Aberdeen

ISBN 0 904484 01 7

CONTENTS

Editorial   vii

1 1491-1500: *Decennium Mirabile* or *Zwischen den Zeiten?*   1

2 The Place of Theology in the Foundation of the University   11

3 "The Fear of the LORD is the Beginning of Wisdom": The Biblical Warrant for a University and Much Else Besides   19

4 The Fear of the Lord - Then and Now   29

5 The Wisdom of God and the Wisdom of the World. Theology and the University   37

6 Study Rooted in Devotion - the Aberdeen Theological Tradition   44

7 Thomas Reid on the Objectivity of Morals   54

8 Between Legalism and Liberalism: Wisdom in Christian Ethics   64

9 Marrying Wisdom and Witness. A New Foundation for Practical Theology   72

10 Aberdeen University and the Study of Religions   81

11 Theology and the idea of University   93

12 Notes   103

LIST OF CONTRIBUTORS

Professor Jaroslav Pelikan
Sterling Professor, Department of History at Yale University, and President of the American Academy of Arts and Sciences, Gifford Lecturer, University of Aberdeen, 1992-93

Dr G Patrick Edwards
Senior Lecturer in Classics, University of Aberdeen

Professor William Johnstone
Professor of Hebrew and Semitic Languages, University of Aberdeen

Professor I Howard Marshall
Professor of New Testament Exegesis, University of Aberdeen

Dr Brian Rosner
Lecturer in New Testament, University of Aberdeen

Dr Ian Bradley
Lecturer in Church History and Practical Theology, University of Aberdeen

Professor David AS Fergusson
Professor of Systematic Theology, University of Aberdeen

Dr Iain R Torrance
Lecturer in Systematic and Practical Theology, University of Aberdeen

Dr William F Storrar
Lecturer in Practical Theology, University of Aberdeen

Professor Jan Milič Lochman
Emeritus Professor of Theology and Rector Magnificus, 1981-83, University of Basle

Professor James A Thrower
Professor of the History of Religions, University of Aberdeen

EDITORIAL

The Quincentenary of the University affords an excellent vantage point from which both to survey what has been as well as the prospect of what is yet to be; and this volume of essays seeks to make a contribution to the endeavour, tracing something of the story of theology at Aberdeen University, then, as a founding Faculty and now, as a new and thriving entity, Divinity with Religious Studies. The high watermark of 1995 very properly bids all who love their *Alma Mater* to pause, reflect and recollect, not in the spirit of sentimental longing for the halcyon days of yesteryear but, rather - having taken the backward look - to draw strength and encouragement the better to take on the undoubted challenges of the future - post the millennium. To employ the parlance of the television era - we are in a situation of rewind and fast forward, which is very much what current life in the modern university feels like.

The essays, as will be seen from the list of contributors, have been produced by current members of the academic staff, "topped and tailed" by two of our honorary graduates, Professors Jaroslav Pelikan and Jan Milič Lochman whose respective chapters set the undertaking in the larger perspective of a wide-angle view. Having located 1495 in the impressive context of great figures and events leading to 1500, the focus homes in more particularly upon the earliest founding days of the infant King's College, a tiny institution, 36 souls strong, from which acorn has sprung the community of 10,000 which exists today. Through the vicissitudes of its 500 years of existence there could not but have been colossal changes to the *modus vivendi* of the University but in Patrick Edwards' "*The Place of Theology in the Foundation*" the thread is finely woven linking academic endeavour, spirituality, community, work and worship which emerges again and again in the remaining chapters.

One unchanging constant is the motto of Aberdeen University, (which we have adopted as the sub-title of this volume) - *Initium Sapientiae Timor Domini*; and the chapters by William Johnstone and Howard Marshall set out to explore with scholarly care facets of what that motto may mean for us now, drawn from biblical and historical contexts. Brian Rosner, in imaginative vein, turns his New Testament scholarship to the addressing of the question, not of what theology can do for the University - but rather of what the University can do for theology, an engaging and persuasive venture.

Conscious as we are especially at this time of the centuries that have passed since 1495, the next two contributions from Ian Bradley and David Fergusson, in differing ways bridge the long gap of the years from then till now, Bradley concentrating via the overarching theme of spirituality and "*Study rooted in devotion*", upon a number of outstanding figures who successively graced the University's scene with their learning and piety; and Fergusson, taking as representative figure Thomas Reid, to focus the gaze upon the perennially new question of moral realism and relativism. From that point Iain Torrance then, in natural extension, addresses the sexual ethical maze in which the Church of Scotland, in common with society as a whole, currently finds itself; offering, by way of Michael Polanyi (Gifford Lecturer at Aberdeen in the 1950s) a new way of approach which bids fair to avoid the twin pitfalls of legalistic conservatism and unbridled radicalism, while still honouring the gospel imperatives.

In the last section of the volume, broadening the vision again, William Storrar encourages the reader both to keep faith with the Wisdom of the University's motto down the years and to engage with the call to the believer to the once and future task of mission in the world. The world view and "*The Study of World Religions*" in relation to Aberdeen University by James Thrower reflects, again, an old but new emphasis, which finds expression in the current departmental title of Divinity with Religious Studies, evidence of the proper and happy marrying of formerly quite distinct disciplines. That this contributes to the strengthening of the total academic endeavour there can be no doubt, which accounts for the confident spirit with which the Quincentenary is approached.

The volume concludes, continuing the motif of motto, with a positive and hopeful contribution from Jan Milič Lochman, but this time the theme is the analysis of the motto of his own University of Basle, which finds universal application in the aim which it affirms: "The obtaining by God's gift and assiduous study of the pearl of knowledge". Without any difficulty at all one could put that statement into the mouth of William Elphinstone and one can hear it still echoed today in the theological study pursued in this ancient institution.

I would wish to express my great indebtedness and sincere thanks to Mrs Rachel Hart, Secretary to Christ's College, whose contribution was quite invaluable in bringing the volume to successful completion.

Living and working amid the turbulence of the present in the university sector in Britain, it is easy to forget that our University has been here for a very long time and to bewail current anxieties, unmindful of the fact that change has been an almost ever-present constant. Even if it were not so, there should be and there always are certain fixed points from which from time to time to chart a course. *Initium Sapientiae Timor Domini* is one such and this volume of reflection is offered, in solidarity with our honoured past, in recognition of the continuing task, and as earnest of what is yet to be in days to come. Deo Gloria.

Alan Main, Master of Christ's College.

1

1491-1500: *DECENNIUM MIRABILE* OR *ZWISCHEN DEN ZEITEN* ?

Jaroslav Pelikan

It has been said that everyone has twenty-twenty vision by hindsight. But in the historian this tendency becomes an occupational hazard, if not indeed an occupational disease. In a book published in 1931, Herbert Butterfield even gave it a label, which has stuck to it.[1] Historians of ideas seem to have a special propensity to engage in 'the Whig interpretation of history'. Thus the historian of science is tempted to suppose that an experiment or series of experiments could not have come out any other way than it did, and then to 'explain' the process that led to it. And historians of philosophy or theology are tempted to take a system - often, for some reason, it turns out to be their own system - as such an outcome, and then to interpret the entire history of hitherto existing thought as a prelude to it; as Faust's research assistant, Wagner, puts it:

"... es ist ein groß Ergetzen,
Sich in den Geist der Zeiten zu versetzen;
Zu schauen, wie vor uns ein weiser Mann gedacht,
Und wie wir's dann zuletzt so herrlich weit gebracht"
[It is very gratifying to transport oneself into the spirit
of the times, to look at what some wise man before our
time once thought, and then to see what wonderful
progress we have finally made][2]

- words that Karl Barth has quoted and parodied to great effect in the introduction to my favourite among his works, *Die protestantische Theologie im 19. Jahrhundert.*[3]

The temptation of the Whig interpretation of the history of theology becomes all but irresistible when the topic for interpretation is the final decade of the fifteenth century in the Latin West, in the precise middle of which came the founding by Bishop William Elphinstone of King's College in Old Aberdeen, which eventually became the University of Aberdeen, under a

2

bull issued by Pope Alexander VI on 10 February 1495: eighty
years after the execution of Jan Hus at the Council of Constance
and fifty years before the convoking of the Council of Trent. As
it happens, in that portentous decade each of the four years on
either side of 1495 marks some event that was to shape the history of theology throughout Christendom, and of theological
education at Aberdeen and elsewhere. Having devoted a sub-
stantial portion of the fourth volume of my history of doctrine
to an examination of the theological primary sources of this
period,[4] I would suggest, with full awareness of its arbitrariness
and of its artificiality, that a chronological review of those four
years before 1495 and four years after 1495 does serve to put
this Quincentenary into context.[5]

1491: birth of Ignatius Loyola

One of the most striking features of Bishop Elphinstone's foundation was its close tie to the Dominican Order: "[T]he first to
obtain a doctorate of Theology at Aberdeen was the Dominican, John Adamson ... There were other Dominicans, too, who
began their theological studies before King's College was built".[6]
That close tie is a reminder of the dominance of the religious
orders in the study and teaching of theology before the Protestant Reformation, which was continued and deepened by the
Society of Jesus and its founder, St Ignatius Loyola. Although
Loyola is, for good reason, remembered - and either celebrated
or abhorred - for the role of the Society of Jesus in furthering
the Counter-Reformation, the central theme of his work and (to
borrow a phrase from Schleiermacher) 'the melody of his life',
was reformation through education. As a brilliant recent study
by John W O'Malley has pointed out, it was this "new, international education style", with its fundamental principle of a "com-
patibility between an education in 'humane letters' on the one
hand and in Aristotelian philosophy/science and Thomistic theology on the other",[7] that set Loyola's movement apart and ac-
counted for its success. In the event, it was in response to the
Protestant Reformation and in the campaign to recoup the losses
incurred as a result of the Reformation that Jesuit education,
both theological education and lay education, would carry out

its mission. But it is important for a proper historical under-standing of Loyola's ministry - and therefore also for an under-standing of his significance for the Quincentenary of King's College - to keep in mind that the fundamental impulse under-lying this educational outlook was the Christian Renaissance and not only, or even primarily, the Catholic Counter-Reforma-tion. For the Renaissance created the intellectual and theologi-cal climate within which both King's College, Old Aberdeen as a Papal foundation and the Society of Jesus as a Papal founda-tion - and King's College, Old Aberdeen as a Reformed institu-tion - pursued their educational missions.

1492: beginning of Hebrew study by Johannes Reuchlin

As the historian of the University of Aberdeen has noted, "it is remarkable how quickly its Faculties of Theology and the lib-eral Arts responded to the new challenge of the humanists, with ... their introduction of Greek, and a little later, Hebrew stud-ies".[8] For in spite of the massive authority of the Old Testament for Christian teaching,[9] throughout most of its history the de-velopment of Christian theology has been largely innocent of the original language of the Hebrew Bible. Origen of Alexan-dria, arguably the greatest scholar in Christian history, knew Hebrew, and so did Jerome, whom Augustine called a '*vir trilinguis*' because of his mastery of Latin, Greek, and Hebrew; but they were highly exceptional in their own time and even afterwards. Under the heading '*Hebraica Veritas*' the late Beryl Smalley has described the historical process by which the later Middle Ages began coming to the conclusion, as she paraphrases the thought of Roger Bacon, that "knowledge of Hebrew and Chaldean [Aramaic] is indispensable to an understanding of the idiom and rhythm, and hence of the meaning of the Old Testa-ment".[10] Nevertheless, that conclusion did not achieve anything resembling universal acceptance in the Church; and it remained for the Renaissance, as represented by Johannes Reuchlin, to make the scientific study of Hebrew a mandatory component of the scholarly equipment of the Christian interpreter of the Old Testament, and then for the Reformation to incorporate this study into the curriculum of preparation not only for the scholar but for the minister. Reuchlin, as Briggs put it, "laid the foundation for Hebrew scholarship among Christians by publishing the first Hebrew grammar and lexicon, combined in the work *De rudimentis hebraicis* (1506)".[11] Reuchlin first undertook that study in 1492, and his epitaph bears witness to its importance for him: "He restored the elegant Muses and brought both the Hebrew and the Greek tongue back from extinction".[12] The use of his work, also at King's College, Aberdeen, as a result of the purchase of his *Vocabularius breviloquus* by John Vaus,[13] is evidence for the far-reaching importance of this 'sacred philology' and for its 'positive contributions' to both Renaissance and Reformation theology.[14]

1493: birth of Paracelsus

Commenting on the original design of the University in the minds of Bishop Elphinstone and King James IV, its historian has suggested 'that James would have seen the establishment of a Faculty of Medicine at Aberdeen as a golden opportunity to narrow the gap between the theory and practice of medicine in Scotland'. And if there is reason to question his further suggestion that 'the religious ethos of the age encouraged an attitude of passive resignation towards suffering and death, which were accepted as God's will, so that while benefactors were prepared to endow altars, they were less prepared to provide salaries for mediciners at universities', the conclusion he draws from this dubious premise is a correct one: "the Church's official attitude towards the teaching of medicine at the universities ... had long remained ambivalent".[15] That 'ambivalence' is well illustrated in the historical coincidence of what I have just called 'Renaissance and Reformation theology' with the birth of Theophrastus Bombastus Paracelsus von Hohenheim, a major figure in the history of medicine, and a few decades later in the career of Michael Servetus, who is best remembered for denying the doctrine of the Trinity but who should also be remembered for having anticipated by precisely three-quarters of a century William Harvey's discovery of the circulation of the blood. Thus, as seen from the perspective of later history, one of the most ambiguous issues in the theology and theological education of the sixteenth century is its relation to the natural sciences. Although the Protestant Reformers with some justification believed themselves to be, by their study of the Bible, liberating the study of nature from the shackles of scholastic Aristotelianism, the 'ambivalence' was not put to rest on either side of the division coming out of the Reformation: for reasons I have never been able to discern with precision, Roman Catholicism faced its crisis in the field of physics in the case of Galileo, while Protestantism, in the case of Darwin, was challenged by biology instead.

1494: birth of Suleiman the Magnificent

That 'ambivalence' in the position of medicine within the medieval university may also have had some connection to another aspect of "the state of medical education in Europe" at the time of the founding of the University of Aberdeen, the "large corpus of Islamic medical lore [that] had also been translated and absorbed into western culture", which seems also to have been reflected in "the early medical books at King's College" and in the curriculum of its Faculty of Medicine.[16] Now that our knowledge of Islamic intellectual history is finally beginning to catch up with the state of the source material, it is becoming possible to give attention to the place of Islam within European thought during the centuries preceding the Renaissance and Reformation. Indeed, the three-way dialogue between Judaism, Christianity, and Islam in the Middle Ages presents us with a case study of how the monotheisms of the Book related themselves both to philosophy and to science, and thus also to one another. As Etienne Gilson put it with characteristic directness in his Gifford Lectures at the University of Aberdeen for 1931, "*La philosophie des chrétiens n'est pas la seule à se réclamer de la Bible et des Grecs: un philosophe juif, tel que Maïmonide; un philosophe musulman, tel qu'Avicenne, ont poursuivi de leur côté une oeuvre parallèle à celle que les Chrétiens eux-mêmes poursuivent*".[17] Suleiman the Magnificent, born in the year before the foundation of King's College, would lead the Ottoman forces to the conquest of Belgrade in 1521 and the defeat of the Hungarians at Mohacs in 1526. The siege of Vienna by his armies in 1529 was part of Reformation history; for the Diet of Augsburg convoked in 1530, at which the Augsburg Confession was presented, had on its agenda the dual threat of the Turks and the Protestants. The events of the late twentieth century suggest that these issues still represent unfinished business.

1496: lectures of John Colet at Oxford

Although, also in Elphinstone's mind, "the defence of Christian orthodoxy was seen in itself to be one of the essential functions of any university", Elphinstone "had become increasingly open to Renaissance and humanist ideas, and it is certain that he wished to reflect all that was best in this movement, whether French, Italian or English, when initiating his own Arts course in Aberdeen".[18] Two decades before Luther's posting of the ninety-five theses, those two interests, in the defence of orthodoxy and in biblical humanism, could be seen as congruent by Elphinstone - and by John Colet at Oxford. In his lectures at Oxford Colet criticised late medieval scholasticism and espoused a humanistic method in the exegesis of the New Testament, including an emphasis on the need to be able to expound it on the basis of the original Greek text.[19] By the twenty-twenty vision of hindsight from the middle of the sixteenth century, this may correctly be seen as an anticipation of the hermeneutical emphases of Luther and Calvin, but only if one does not neglect to note Colet's (and Elphinstone's) impeccable Catholic orthodoxy. And by hindsight from later centuries, the use of the universities, and specifically of their Faculties of Theology, as a venue to challenge all orthodoxy, Catholic or Protestant, in the name of the most recent biblical scholarship was to become a major source of tension between the leadership of the churches and the leadership of the very universities on which the churches were dependent for their intellectual and scholarly leadership. The King's patronage of King's College was a potential source of such tension in the future, also for the universities of Scotland, "although [Macfarlane reminds us] it is significant that at Aberdeen ... the University resisted the threat to its constitution".[20]

1497: birth of Philip Melanchthon

At first impression, even to a scholar as well versed in late medieval history as Leslie J Macfarlane, it seems quite striking or even strange that despite Bishop Elphinstone's having "become increasingly open to Renaissance and humanist ideas", "the Bible and ... the *Sentences* of Peter Lombard ... were the only two major textbooks allowed" in the Faculty of Theology at King's College at the end of the fifteenth and the beginning of the sixteenth century.[21] The list of commentators on the *Sentences,* which has long since passed the two thousand mark and which continues to grow with new manuscript findings,[22] includes such names as Albertus Magnus, Thomas Aquinas, Bonaventure, Duns Scotus, William of Ockham, Gregory of Rimini - and Jan Hus and Martin Luther. Thus it is possible to trace the history of a doctrine in medieval systematic theology from the twelfth to the sixteenth century by comparing these commentaries. But in the compilation of these commentaries the decade of the founding of the University of Aberdeen and the decades immediately following it do indeed fall '*zwischen den Zeiten*', and that in two contrasting ways. On the Roman Catholic side of the great divide that was about to form so soon after that founding date, the period of the Counter-Reformation (or, perhaps better, of the 'Catholic Reformation') saw the steady ascendancy of the *Summa Theologica* of Thomas Aquinas to the position of dominance in systematic theology that it has gone on occupying into the twentieth century, thanks to such endorsements as the encyclical *Aeterni Patris* issued by Pope Leo XIII on 4 August 1879. But on the Protestant side, the sixteenth and seventeenth centuries were to witness a veritable explosion of manuals of systematic theology. Of these, John Calvin's *Institutes of the Christian Religion* was in many respects the most important, but the first was the *Loci communes* published by Philip Melanchthon (grandnephew of Reuchlin) in 1521. Its outline followed that of the Epistle to the Romans, on which Melanchthon lectured with the aid of the philological methodology of biblical humanism.

1498: coming of Erasmus to Oxford

Although each of the two preceding dates involves significant figures in the history of this 'biblical humanism', Colet and Melanchthon, pride of place in that history belongs to Desiderius Erasmus, who, as it happens, is also the most important biblical humanist for the history of King's College in Old Aberdeen. Its tie to him was the man whom we must designate as, after Bishop William Elphinstone and King James IV, the most decisive figure in the founding of King's College, Hector Boece.[23] Elphinstone, as Macfarlane says,

> "... invited Hector Boece from Paris in 1497. This young Dundonian had recently incepted in Arts at Paris and was then reading (i.e. teaching) Philosophy at Montaigu College there. But he was also an elegant writer of Renaissance prose and verse and a friend of Erasmus, who had once been his fellow student at Montaigu and with whom he still kept up a correspondence ... It seems most likely to have been [William Elphinstone's kinsman, Adam Elphinstone] who drew the bishop's attention either to Boece's classical gifts or to Erasmus' prefatory letter to Boece in his *De casa natalitia Jesu* ... Boece's link with Montaigu College was able to give the University of Aberdeen the intellectual and spiritual direction which Elphinstone wished it to be given."[24]

Both in Theology and in Arts, the University of Aberdeen has continued to bear the mark of Boece's Erasmian humanism, which found a worthy twentieth-century heir in the learned editor of *A Glossary of Later Latin to 600 A.D.*, published by the Clarendon Press of Oxford University Press in 1949, Alexander Souter, Regius Professor of Humanity at Aberdeen from 1911 to 1937, whose portrait hangs in Marischal College.[25] And, as other essays in this volume show, biblical scholarship at Aberdeen has repeatedly demonstrated its debt to this intellectual lineage.

1499: death of Marsilio Ficino

But it was not only by his biblical scholarship that Hector Boece left his mark on both the Faculty of Arts and the Faculty of

Theology in Old Aberdeen. To borrow one last time from Leslie
Macfarlane, while at Aberdeen, as at Paris, "the staple fare of
the Arts course in the late fifteenth and early sixteenth centuries
... remained the logical, physical, and metaphysical works of
Aristotle", it was also the case that, "schooled with Erasmus in
the Standonck tradition, Boece shared with him that rare combination of a deep love of classical literature, of Christian
Platonism and social concern which they had absorbed from
their humanist masters at Paris".[26] If, having earlier quoted the
Gifford Lectures at Aberdeen by Etienne Gilson, I may be permitted to quote the opening sentence from my own Gifford
Lectures at Aberdeen,

> "It remains one of the most momentous linguistic con-
> vergences in the entire history of the human mind and
> spirit that the New Testament happens to have been
> written in Greek - not in the Hebrew of Moses and the
> prophets, nor in the Aramaic of Jesus and his disciples,
> nor yet in the Latin of the *imperium Romanum*, but in
> the Greek of Socrates and Plato, or at any rate in a rea-
> sonably accurate facsimile thereof, disguised and even
> disfigured though this was in the *Koine* by the interven-
> ing centuries of Hellenistic usage."[27]

Despite the vigorous efforts of such scholars as my late mentor,
Father Georges Florovsky, to exorcise the Platonic elements from
Eastern Orthodox theology, even Adolf von Harnack, with all
his antipathy to 'the Hellenisation of the Gospel', had to admit
that there were what he called, characteristically using a
Goethean phrase, 'elements of elective affinity [*wahlverwandte
Elemente*]' between Christianity and [Neo-]Platonism.[28] It is
arguable that the creative 'mainstream' of the development of
Christian theology from Clement of Alexandria to Augustine to
John the Scot to Marsilio Ficino to Ralph Cudworth to Friedrich
Schleiermacher has been that 'Christian Platonism', with the
'Christian Aristotelianism' of St John of Damascus, St Thomas
Aquinas, and Johann Gerhard providing the tools for the peri-
odic systematisations and codifications of doctrine. Also in this
respect, then, the Quincentenary being commemorated in this
volume bears a significance, both symbolic and intrinsic, that

carries beyond Old Aberdeen and Scotland to Christendom as a whole, and beyond that *decennium mirabile* to all the decades and centuries of the history of Christian theology and Christian theological education.

2

THE PLACE OF THEOLOGY IN THE FOUNDATION OF THE UNIVERSITY

G Patrick Edwards

The University of Aberdeen, like her senior sisters at St Andrews and Glasgow, belongs to a group of more than thirty universities founded in Europe during the 15th century. Almost without exception they were established by Church authorities, empowered by a Papal Bull, and they shared a common approach to the traditional areas of study, including theological learning. Latin was the universal language of the Church, of law, and of scholarship and education, so that the movement of students and teachers from one European university to another could take place with relative ease; and the institutions themselves were set up along similar lines, with common features in their constitutions, degrees, offices and organisation. These universities were born into a theocentric age, in which the supremacy of Christendom and of the Catholic religion was evident at every level of society.[1]

This situation is reflected in the series of foundation documents that have survived from Aberdeen University's first three or four decades. A contemporary (1495) copy of King James IV's original letter of supplication to Pope Alexander VI, petitioning for a University to be established in Old Aberdeen, still survives in the Vatican archives. Although this was formally submitted in the name of the Scottish King, it had doubtless been drawn up by William Elphinstone who presented it in person at Rome on 6 February 1495. Dr Leslie Macfarlane paints an unforgettable picture of Elphinstone's visit to Rome and the procedure that would be followed for a meeting of this kind, culminating in the Pope's decision to grant or withhold permission for the new institution to be established.[2]

In the event the response to the petition was favourable, and Elphinstone was able to make the long journey back to Aberdeen bringing with him the Papal Bull dated 10 February 1495, which has ever since remained in the University's possession. There are many statements in this document that are relevant to theology and the need for theological study. The ignorance of the populace in the north and north-eastern parts of Scotland is said to be so great that "suitable men cannot be found, whether for preaching the word of God to the people of those parts or even for administering the sacraments of the church." The Bull refers to King James IV's hope that "there may be a teeming fountain in that place, from whose fulness may drink all the faithful in Christ, from whatever quarter they come flocking in, desiring to be adorned with learning and virtues." The concluding part of the Bull begins: "We, therefore, who seek by all the means we can the exaltation of the Catholic faith, the salvation of souls and the advantage and profit of all the faithful, favourably disposed to these supplications, do of our apostolic authority, by the tenor of these presents, appoint and ordain that there be henceforth and flourish in all times to come a university in the said city of Old Aberdeen, and that a university of general study should exist as well in theology, canon and civil law, medicine and the liberal arts, as in every other lawful faculty."[3]

While it may be gratifying to find that theology is put first in the list of faculties in this founding document, it has to be admitted that the details, whether academic or practical, of what is to be established, are vague. Both the letter of supplication and the Bull expressed hopes and aspirations rather than undertakings and commitments. Nevertheless the exchange of these documents was highly important: the project could not have gone forward without the Papal approval which the King had sought and which the Bull embodied. William Elphinstone was well aware of what this approval would now require, and he was soon devoting himself to planning financial provision, finding physical space, and appointing staff for the new university.

One of the earliest appointments to be made was that of Hector Boece to be Aberdeen University's first teacher of liberal arts. Boece himself tells how on arrival in Aberdeen he was made welcome by the canons, some of whom were very learned men. He mentions in particular David Guthrie, professor of Civil and Canon Law, and James Ogilvie, theologian and teacher. These men "gifted with extraordinary mental powers, attracted the admiration of all who heard them by the eloquence of which they were masters, and with which they taught as professors or preachers, or pleaded as advocates. They worked with all their effort at expounding to crowded audiences, the one the sacred writings, the other pontifical (canon) law."[4]

A document dated 17 September 1505 and drawn up for Elphinstone by Alexander Galloway, clerk of the Diocese of Aberdeen and later to become Rector of Kinkell by Inverurie, is more explicit. It details various financial arrangements for support "of the doctors and masters reading, and of certain persons studying, in the faculties of theology, canon and civil law, medicine and arts", and confirms that the Bishop has "erected, founded and endowed in the foresaid University of the foresaid town of Old Aberdeen a collegiate church or college ... in honour and reverence of the Holy and Indivisible Trinity, Father, Son and Holy Spirit, and of the undefiled Virgin Mary, the Mother of the same God and of our Lord Jesus Christ, and of all his saints and elect." The purpose in setting up such a community, almost monastic in its organisation, is that its members "may have the ability and energy to be unencumbered in devoting their attention more honourably, safely, freely and quietly, as becomes ministers of God and worshippers in the Catholic faith, for which end they are for ever appointed, and that they may eat all together in a collegiate manner in one house, and sleep and rest under one roof."

This shared, worshipping life was the rule for the whole academic community, not just those members who were teaching or studying theology. But it is clear that, for the theologians particularly, their daily routine and their theological study or teaching were of a piece, and they had their special part to play in the institution's ecclesiastical life. The college, as established in 1505, was to be for 36 persons, "of whom the first shall be a master in theology, if such can conveniently be had, or else a licentiate in the same faculty (with strict examination of the same), who within a year shall cause himself to be raised to the degree of master in the same faculty, who also ought to be called principal of the said college ..."

The other five "staff" appointments were for teachers in canon law, civil law, medicine, and arts, - the latter to have the title of Subprincipal -, and another master in arts who is to instruct the junior members in (Latin) grammar. Thus each of the "faculties" listed in the 1495 Bull were catered for by one teacher (counting the two divisions of Law separately). Next come five Masters of Arts who are to study theology (it is to be noted that there is no parallel provision for students of law or medicine); these postgraduate students are to "be maintained for that time only which is necessarily required for a Licence in theology, namely for seven years only".

Then there are to be "thirteen poor scholars or clerks", who are to study Arts for not more than the three and a half years required to attain the master's degree. This group of Arts students was important for theological studies because "the most able and of best disposition" from among them, on completing the M.A., might be chosen to fill any vacancy that occurred among the five students of theology. This must have been a keenly sought privilege, since while only three or four of the thirteen scholars might attain the M.A. in any one year, the seven years of study for theology would mean that in some years there were no vacancies to be filled.

These thirteen have brought the complement of the College so far to a total of 24. The remaining twelve members had particular responsibility for worship in the college chapel: "eight prebendaries established in priests' orders, skilled and taught in Gregorian chant" and if possible having other musical accomplishments; and finally "four youths or boys, poor but amenable, taught at least in Gregorian chant." The eight shall be obliged to study in one of the faculties, and shall include a cantor or choirmaster who is to be in charge of the choir and the rota of altar-servers; a sacrist to look after bell-ringing, altar-cloths and frontals, candles, books, vessels and vestments, not to mention cleaning the chapel and taking care of the college clock; and last but not least among the eight there must be appointed one who is skilled in playing the organ.

Such was the ecclesiastical and domestic setting in which the study of theology was pursued during Aberdeen University's earliest years. It is already clear from the number of members engaged in its pursuit, notably from the provision for five graduates in Arts to study for the Licentiate in theology, that the subject had a special importance, and this extended to practice as well as theory. "The principal of the said college, when he is in health, is to read in theology on every lecturing day and to preach the Word of God to the people six times in the year. The said students in theology, when they are in health, are likewise obliged, after being advanced to the degree of Bachelor, to read in theology and likewise preach to the people six times in the year, and before their promotion to the said degree of Bachelor to preach in Latin by turn in the chapter of the said college, all the students being assembled, at the order of the principal master thereof, on every Sunday throughout the whole year" and on certain festivals.

The document of 1505 which contains these provisions was itself given Papal approval, by Julius II in May 1506. About a quarter of a century later a "revised foundation", embodying Elphinstone's later wishes, was drawn up by Bishop Gavin Dunbar and confirmed by Pope Clement VII in June 1531. Membership of the College was now enlarged from 36 to 42, by adding a sixth student in theology, three priests to study canon and civil law and to fulfil certain ecclesiastical obligations, and two more boys to be taught singing and to study in one of the faculties.

It might be supposed that these "institutional plans" represent an ideal, perhaps set out on paper to satisfy the ecclesiastical authorities, rather than a reality that was ever achieved. One may compare the situation at Glasgow, where Divinity teaching in the pre-Reformation period (1451 to 1560 in their case) has been dismissed by one scholar in just a few lines: "There is specific provision in the Bull of Pope Nicholas V, by which the University was established, for theological study. There is, however, no clear evidence of the effective existence of a Theological Faculty in the pre-Reformation period."[5]

At Aberdeen there is in fact plenty of evidence that theological studies were alive and active in the early decades of the 16th century. Hector Boece himself describes how many of the earliest students who graduated from the University were "skilled in theology and in civil and canon law." He mentions by name John Gryson, Robert Lisle [Lyle] and Alexander Hall, who became "members of the order of Friar Preachers and theologians of tried knowledge and piety" as well as John Adam [Adamson], "a man of rare piety and learning, who was the first in Aberdeen to reach in that faculty the crowning honour of master", and who already, when Boece was writing about 1520, had become Provincial or Principal of this order in Scotland.[6] A letter written by Boece to Erasmus in May 1528 mentions with pride how a learned visitor from the continent had been delighted to see students of theology at Aberdeen - "the remotest nook of the world" as Boece calls it - with Erasmus's *Paraphrase of Christ's Gospel* constantly in their hands.[7] This work had been published as recently as 1522-24.

Another remarkable piece of evidence for the quality of theological teaching in these early years is to be found in a manuscript containing some lectures of William Hay, which is preserved in the University Library. Hay had studied with Boece at Paris in the 1490s, and came to Aberdeen in 1505 to be Subprincipal of King's College. When Boece died in 1536 Hay succeeded him as Principal for about six years. The notes are dated 1533-35 and contain the second half of a theological course on the seven sacraments. The subjects covered by the surviving lectures are Unction, Order, and Marriage, the last of which has been admirably edited and translated.[8] Hay followed lines of argument laid down in the 12th century by Peter Lombard, the "Master of the Sentences", whose expositions were a regular basis for much theological teaching, in medieval universities; but he also cites, usually with commendable accuracy, various classical authors ranging from Hesiod to Apuleius, as well as many Church Fathers and medieval theologians. He is not averse to raising contemporary examples and controversies, such as the divorce of Henry VIII of England from Catherine of Aragon, brought about in 1533. It is interesting to see with what frankness and ease Hay discusses some of the more intimate aspects of the marriage relationship. In general we get the impression that here was a school which taught the orthodox line of the church of its time: the orderly exposition of well-established doctrine was more important than novelty or original criticism.

The period following the deaths of Boece, William Hay, and others of that first generation of teachers at King's College, seems to have been one of decline. A Chancellor's inspection or 'visitation' was carried out in 1549 by a group of cathedral canons led by the now venerable Alexander Galloway, whose association with King's, as we have seen, went back to the days of Elphinstone, and who was now Rector of the University for the fourth time. Their report and recommendations were submitted to the Bishop as Chancellor, and they make strange reading: the professors are told that they must resume teaching within nine days (we wonder what else they were doing). The students of theology had become rebellious, ignoring the requirement that they must seek entry to the priesthood: they are instructed to remedy this at once, and to get their hair cut and beards trimmed, on pain of excommunication! We see an insistence on the old system as laid down in the provisions of the founding documents. Everybody is to hear the Foundation read four times a year. No doubt the rot was stopped, for a time.[9]

But in Scotland and many other places, the fresh wind of Reform was already blowing through the academic and ecclesiastical scene. The old guard at King's were swept aside in 1569, and their patterns of teaching and communal life were replaced by new ones. Continuity with the past was recognised, but also the necessity of a break from it, as is evident from the introduction to James VI's New Foundation for King's, dating from the late 1580s: "Although the foundations of this splendid work - laid by our forbears with the counsel of the Bishop of Aberdeen - are not to be regretted, yet, since that age tolerated many things which do not conform with the clear light of the Gospel in these our own times ... we have reckoned it a worthwhile reward for our trouble that we can prescribe for this our gymnasium ... that law which seems best able to serve the glory of God, the well-being of the church," and so on.[10]

Similar 'New Foundation' documents embodying the intended reforms had been received by other Scottish colleges around this time, and the founding Charter of Marischal, dated

2 April 1593, was to follow the same lines, sometimes even the same wording, as at King's. In both institutions the Principal must be "an upright and godly man ... well versed in the scriptures, able to unfold the mysteries of faith and the hidden treasures of the word of God. He must also be skilled and learned in languages, and especially in Hebrew and in Syriac" (i.e. Aramaic). Sunday was hardly a day of rest for the Principal at King's: he was required every week, over and above his College duties, to preach to the congregation of St Machar's Cathedral. The students at both Colleges also were kept hard at it. The Marischal charter runs: "Every Lord's Day, we desire that in each of the classes the reading of a sacred Sunday lesson be given from the Greek New Testament, so that at six o'clock in the morning the first class shall have read to it by its teacher St Luke's Gospel, the second class the Acts of the Apostles, the third the Epistle of St. Paul to the Romans, and the fourth the Epistle to the Hebrews, and that at four o'clock in the afternoon each teacher shall examine his students upon the same lesson."[11]

If, a hundred years after he had brought back his prized Foundation Bull of 1495, the spirit of William Elphinstone had returned to Aberdeen, he would have been astonished to find not one University but two, both tiny institutions, and neither of them owing allegiance to the Church of Rome, but vociferously hostile towards it. At King's, in the beloved Chapel where he himself, Hector Boece and others lay buried, his prescribed round of divine services had ceased. But he would not have failed to observe that the leaders of the new ecclesiastical regime in Scotland, and the teachers at King's and Marischal colleges alike, were passionately addicted to biblical scholarship and divine learning. Aberdeen University had seen a turbulent and at times tumultuous first century, but the study of theology was set upon a sure foundation; it would prove to be a robust and vigorous activity through the many more troubles and upheavals that lay ahead.

3

'THE FEAR OF THE LORD IS THE BEGINNING OF WISDOM': THE BIBLICAL WARRANT FOR A UNIVERSITY AND MUCH ELSE BESIDES
(illustrated with reference to the work of William Robertson Smith)[1]

William Johnstone

One of the logos officially adopted by the University of Aberdeen for its quincentenary includes the motto, devised at the fusion of King's and Marischal Colleges in 1860 when the modern University was formed, *initium sapientiae timor domini*. As a consequence, since session 1992-93, after a gap of 38 years, the University has put its motto back on to the cover of its *Calendar* and the School of Modern Languages, the Department of Mathematical Science, the Computing Centre, the University Library, even the University administration and the Principal himself - to take random examples from my recent internal mail - are all solemnly affirming on their notepaper, "The fear of the LORD is the beginning of wisdom".

What can the University mean by using this motto? Is it merely decoration, a link with the historic past, but a functionless relic, the meaning of which lies safely buried in the obscurity of Latin? I suspect that the University is quite happy to understand, and even to affirm, its motto in a purely historical way. Without inquiring too closely into what the words might mean, it is content to acknowledge that the fear of the LORD *was* in its beginnings: we have a Papal Bull to prove it; our founding bishop lies here among us. As the University celebrates its 500th anniversary it takes pleasure and, indeed, pride in looking back at its past, and that past includes religious beginnings.

But this motto chosen by the University to be at the heart of its celebrations is also a biblical text which is itself the motto of the Wisdom literature of the Hebrew Bible (Ps. 111:10; cf Prov. 1:7). There are here far-reaching theological implications. The

choice of it thus provides Divinity with Religious Studies with
an unrivalled opportunity to consider theologically questions of
immediate relevance to the institution and to this occasion in its
life. Is its use merely the mouthing of harmless pious sentiments
once traditional in Scotland[2] or can such a motto be credibly
and functionally affirmed in the pluralist and secular society of
today?

In the history of the University few have been better placed
to vindicate the claims of biblical truth to be functional in living
contemporary terms than William Robertson Smith (1846-94;
MA Aberdeen 1865; LL.D. 1882; Burnett Lecturer 1888-91).[3]
In one of his earliest essays (written at the age of twenty-two
while he was still a Divinity student at The New College, Edinburgh), Smith could be said to have transposed the University
motto into his own terms in these arresting words: "It is the
business of Christianity to conquer the whole universe to itself
and not least the universe of thought".[4]

Smith was uniquely qualified for the task: when he planned
to enter the competition for the prestigious Ferguson Scholarship, open to graduates of the then all four Scottish universities,
he was initially undecided which of the three areas in which
scholarships were offered - Philosophy, Classics or Mathematics - to compete in, for he was equally accomplished in each (he
finally chose Mathematics).[5] His scholarly range is well expressed by the Principal of the University of Aberdeen of the
time, Sir William Geddes (who as Professor of Greek had earlier taught Smith), at the unveiling of the memorial window to
Smith in King's College Chapel[6] on 31st August 1897:

> "[Smith] showed quality and power placing him high
> among scholars and thinkers, not only of his own age,
> but of any age and time ... [P]robably, he was the only
> one of his time in our country who was able to com-
> mand at one and the same time the Oriental as well as
> the Occidental field of thought ... an ideal editor for a
> world-storehouse of knowledge like the 'Encyclopae-
> dia Britannica' [the ninth edition of which he edited] ...
> To have done so much and to have produced such works,
> in compassing so large a portion of the field of knowl-

edge while still a youth considerably under the seven times seven of 49 which Aristotle regarded as the culminating point of man's intellectual power ...".[7]

The key sphere where Smith sought in the name of Christianity "to conquer the whole universe of thought" was history. The centre of his theological programme was his "scientific proof of the divine character of the Old Testament Scripture".[8] This "proof" necessarily involved the study of history - the history of Semitic religion, which was the subject of his best-known work, *The Religion of the Semites* - in order to display the qualitative difference of the revealed religion of the Hebrew prophets and Christianity from Semitic "heathenism"[9] (the former is *not* the product of a natural process of evolution).

In the study of history, the same data are available to all, believer and unbeliever alike, and provide the meeting ground for all, though a different construction will be put on those data:

> "The fundamental principle of the higher criticism lies in the conception of the organic unity of all history. We must not see in history only a medley of petty dramas involving no higher springs of action than the passions and interests of individuals. History is ... the life and life-work of mankind continually unfolding in one great plan ... .
>
> "... That a unity of plan runs through all history, all must hold who in any sense believe in Providence. But ... to one thinker the organic development of history will mean the unbroken sweep of natural law without one breath of the creative Spirit from on high, while to a higher school of thought the one purpose of history is the purpose of everlasting love, worked out, in, and through human personality, by a personal redeeming God."[10]

There is here a straightforward application of the evangelical faith first learned and embraced by Smith in his father's Free Church Manse at Keig:[11] the God who had made himself known to the lad in frequent bouts of life-threatening illness, awakening unshakeable personal conviction, is the one whom the believer encounters in Scripture and whose working one can discern in the patterns of history.

In this work of historical research the new historical critical methods of studying the Bible seemed to Smith to provide the very tools that were required. The popular perception of these methods in the Britain of the time was that they were deployed by rationalists as instruments with which to attack traditional Christian orthodoxy. Smith saw his task as to rescue the method and apply it in the execution of his programme.[12] To trace the history of Israel's religion from the general level of "Semitic heathenism" to the "positive religion of the prophets" by means of, for example, the analysis of the Pentateuch into its constituent sources, was a duty that Smith felt imposed upon him by his convictions, both as a Christian and as a scholar.

It was here, not surprisingly, that he fell foul of his church. To embrace the view that, for example, Deuteronomy was a legislative programme dependent on the work of the eighth century prophets (the final nub of the libel with which he was charged) seemed to contradict the testimony of Scripture to its own origins and thus to cast doubt on the authority of Scripture itself. Smith occupied the theological high ground throughout the libel process, as he always had done, whether on miracle (*the* miracle is "the incarnation and resurrection of our Lord"),[13] or doctrine (God reveals himself, not facts),[14] or the authority of Scripture. To illustrate but the latter: in his *Answer to the Form of Libel now before the Free Church Presbytery of Aberdeen* (12 February 1878), he draws a striking parallel between Scripture and the Elements in Holy Communion. In the sentence "The Bible is the Word of God", he says, "the sense ... depends on the force of the word *is* ... One school of theologians presses the word as strictly as Lutherans and Romanists do in the famous controversy on the words 'This is my body'. And they press it with as little reason" (p 24). In Reformed Theology, the Bible is no more transubstantially the Word of God than are the Elements of the Sacrament transubstantially the body and blood of the Redeemer.

Part of what was at stake was whether the Confession could be extended, or 'extruded',[15] to deal with such technical matters as dates of composition and numbers of authors. What is notable in Smith is his non-reductionism of traditional belief.

But this belief rests on according a proper priority to God in all things; the Bible and Confession remain ancillary. Smith is adamant about any 'extrusion' of the Confession:[16] authority and infallibility belong not to the words of Scripture but to God alone:

> "the conclusion that Scripture *is* of infallible truth and Divine authority, will be more correctly expressed by saying that Scripture records or conveys to us the infallible and authoritative Word of God.
>
> "... [W]ill it not be objected that this last expression ... leaves an opening for doubt whether the Scripture is a correct and adequate record? By no means, replies the theology of the Reformation, for the Holy Spirit accompanies the Word as it is brought to us in Scripture, with exactly the same testimony which he bare to the Word in the hearts of its first hearers, nay, ... whereby he assured the prophets and apostles that the word which they preached was God's Word, and not their own. The witness of the Spirit does not attach itself to the outward characters of the record (1 Cor. ii.1-5); but testifies directly to the infallible truth of the Divine Word, the spiritual doctrine, the revelation of God Himself, which is the substance of the record."

And he continues in words which show that the controversy - need one say? - is still alive today:

> "Scripture is not the record of a word which was once infallible, but may have been corrupted in transmission. It is the record of a word which still speaks with infallible truth and personal authority to us, in accordance, as Calvin well observes, with the promise, Isa. lix. 21 ...".[17]

After five years of highly charged debate in Presbytery and General Assembly, the libel against Smith could not be sustained. Nonetheless, at the General Assembly of May 1881 he was dismissed from his post not for denial of any fundamental doctrine nor for the application of any illicit critical method but for the lame reason that his work was no longer considered "safe or advantageous" in the task of training ministers for the Free Church.[18]

It is with a sense of presumptuousness that one dissents from

Smith, given the conviction, courage and erudition with which he pursued his goals. I believe Smith is right on the high theological ground that he occupies, and yet I also believe that one must find a different ground on which to carry out Smith's programme of "conquering the universe of thought". Smith was a child of his age: his optimistic thought that a pattern is discernible in history (whether acknowledged as providential or not) strikes an unconvincing note for us at the end of the following century and is quite implausible as a common meeting-ground for our generation. It surely reflects the optimism of the high noon of the Victorian *pax britannica* (as when he writes - even if guardedly - on the superiority and benefits of Western civilisation apparent to the ordinary Arab in Jeddah or the role in the Red Sea area which may yet await Britain).[19] Here, as elsewhere in his work,[20] there is a disturbing foreshortening of perspective.

Where, then, might this alternative meeting-point be found where believer and non-believer find themselves dealing with the same data, confronted by the same phenomena? It is precisely in that area known as Wisdom in the Hebrew Bible, from which the University of Aberdeen has derived its motto.

The link between the University and Wisdom through their respective mottos is highly appropriate. Both begin under royal patronage and for the same reason. In the Hebrew Bible, Solomon is the chief patron and exponent of Wisdom: 1 Kings 3-4 lists the areas of application from law, through the arts of literature and rhetoric, to the sciences of botany and zoology - a veritable university. Proverbs, Ecclesiastes and the Wisdom of Solomon are all attributed to him. The purpose of all this domestic wisdom is to build up an educated, enlightened and cultivated community, dwelling in peace, order and prosperity. For that purpose schools are essential: to produce the civic leaders with the knowledge, integrity and skills required to run his new kingdom and empire, Solomon set up his key educational establishment, King's College, Jerusalem.[21] The motives in setting up King's College, Aberdeen, cannot have been much different.

But the Wisdom literature recognises the complexity and shadow-side of actual human experience. Here we do not need to go into the darker issues so graphically explored in Job and Ecclesiastes; it is enough to use the stock biblical figure of "exile" for the dislocation that lies at the heart of human endeavour. In the Wisdom tales of Daniel 1-6 (or of the Joseph cycle in Genesis), we are transported out of the cosy world of the shared assumptions of the one people, out of an identifiable national community with a clearly articulated self-consciousness, into a world of pluralist culture and competing ideologies. King's College, Jerusalem, is transposed into King's College, Babylon (Dan. 1:5 for the three-year student grant!) (or King's College, Thebes/Memphis, or wherever Joseph was supposed to be functioning); domestic Wisdom is transposed into the realm of international Wisdom.

But in an alien land and in a foreign academic environment the Jew is not at a disadvantage. For Wisdom provides not just strategies but a rationale for survival in an alien, pluralist world. As the very structure of the universe, Wisdom is accessible to empirical observation by all; it can be tapped into the world over. Here is the true sacramentalism: this world in its visible manifestations is but the outer sign of the inner working and purpose of God. Here is Robertson Smith's Providence in its more fundamental self-disclosure - and here are the shared data, the commonly observed phenomena, whether their ultimate, Divine origin and character are acknowledged or not. In local terms, even if the University as a whole is largely indifferent to the truth claims and intellectual instrumentality of its religious past, it cannot get away from it. To say that you're not religious is as futile as the committed whisky drinker saying (as has been said to me) that he never touches water. You may prefer the surface manifestations but you cannot deny the basic medium: secularisation is, in the last analysis, self-contradictory for the truth of human existence as God made it presses in at every turn (Prov. 8!). The Bible affirms that there are very good reasons why the School of Modern Languages, the Department of Mathematical Science, the Computing Centre, the University Library, even, indeed above all, the University Administration should affirm that the fear of the LORD *is* the beginning of wisdom. At the root of all investigation and activity there is order, structure, regularity, forecastable rules of cause and effect, predictable outcomes of planning and action - at least to a degree. This provisional stability, reliability, predictability, that enables the whole academic enterprise - and life in general, of which the academic community is only a tiny segment - is nothing other than an expression of the will of God who has ordered it and made it so. There is a fundamental order in the world around us, and that order is nothing less than the wisdom of God.

Here is a common meeting ground: there is a wisdom that sustains us all - a wisdom accessible to all even if not acknowledged by all for what it is. There is a skill which arises out of knowledge of that order which is shared, which all can attain, whether believer or unbeliever. Thus in King's College, Babylon, Daniel and his fellow-Jews had classmates; they were not the only ones to pass the course and attain wisdom and knowledge. And that is why if I go to the dentist or board an aeroplane I do not ask if the person in charge is a "Christian" (indeed, when a stockbroker I had to consult told me he was a church elder, I rather *lost* confidence!). It is technical competence, not special pleading, for which we look. Secularisation in this sense is the only tolerable form of theocracy: it is an affirmation of the order of the world with which we can co-operate to our benefit, or violate at our peril. And this point is made clear from the structure of our Faculty of Arts *and* Divinity formed in 1989: that twin title has at least this advantage that it stresses what we share in common with all humanity - as well as affirming what is distinctive.

But that is not the whole story. Daniel and the other Jews have another advantage even in "exile" in King's College, Babylon, so that they surpass their classmates. They do not relate themselves merely to faceless nature. The God who has revealed himself in the general revelation of Wisdom has related himself to his people and disclosed himself in the special revelation of their experience. For its full development, general revelation has to be brought into association with special revelation; Wisdom has to be brought into relationship with the Law.[22] It is often maintained that the equation between Wisdom and Law had to wait until the intertestamental period (e.g.,

Ecclus. 24:23). But it is already begun in Deut. 4:5-6:

> "See, I have taught you statutes and ordinances, as
> Yahweh my God commanded me ...You will preserve
> and practise them, for that is your wisdom and your
> understanding in the view of the peoples who, when
> they hear all these statutes, will say, 'Only this great
> nation is a wise and understanding people'."

That is as good an exposition as can be found of "The fear of the
LORD is the beginning of wisdom".

What is the significance of this equation of Wisdom and Law?
For the Jew, the Law is "the marvellous instrument" (Aboth 3:18)
whereby the world was created; the creative instrument in the
unfolding of which the world is sustained; the substance which
the universe sacramentally signifies. It is therefore by the ob-
servance of the Law that the whole created universe is maintained in being. Even in the matters of diet (Dan. 1:8), what we
daily allow ourselves to consume and enjoy, the fabric of God's
creation is being upheld; life-style is instrumental in maintaining God's world. It was by this privileged, creative insight into
the very workings of the universe, and by being prepared to
witness to it in the fiery furnace and the den of lions, that Daniel
and his friends not only surpassed their contemporaries in wisdom and understanding in the alien environment within which
they studied and worked but won their acknowledgement (quite
a tall order for Divinity!).

What is the transposition of this teaching on Wisdom into
the Christian mode, the Gospel in a time of pluralism? For us,
and for all, acknowledged or unacknowledged, the Law has become incarnate: the Law by which the world was made and is
continually being remade has become fully personal in Christ.
In relationship to him, access is granted to the inner workings
of the universe. The incarnation of the cosmic Christ of Ephesians
and Colossians is the counterpart and fulfilment of the immanence of the cosmic Wisdom of Prov. 8.

And what are the implications of this Christian fulfilment?
We share the same data as the world around us. Therefore our
posture cannot be one of separation from the world, especially
not the creation of an in-group for sociological or psychologi-

cal reasons. There can be no seminarisation of Divinity. There can be no false antitheses, no polarisation, no exclusivist either/or. "Christ alone" in cosmic terms is inclusive: he is the head, the summation, in whom all that is partial finds fulfilment, in whom all the parts are included in the whole, in the radical ecumenism of God's universal wisdom. In him the universe truly becomes sacramental, transparent to the inner working of the Divine purpose. An appropriately radical understanding of incarnation is that it is not just a single event but that it is an expression supremely visible in Christ of the immanence of God ("in all their affliction he was afflicted and the angel of his presence brought them salvation", Isa. 63:9).

It is within the universe of life and thought that we must occupy the theological high ground: for it is there that we encounter the God who relates and discloses himself. As Robertson Smith put it in the sentence preceding the one quoted at the beginning: "[T]he scientific development of our apologetic must take the form of a speculative theology in which the subjective consciousness of redemption is objectively evolved into a harmonious theory of the universe as reconciled to God in Christ."

4

THE FEAR OF THE LORD - THEN AND NOW

Howard Marshall

Wisdom and the fear of the Lord

Initium sapientiae timor Domini. So runs the motto of the University. I remember taking part in a student debate in the first week or so of my university career and quoting it as part of a gentle inclusion of some Christian testimony into the proceedings. But the last laugh was with another student who commented from the floor that he had always understood the meaning of the tag to be "The fear of the Dominie is the beginning of wisdom." He was right, of course, for this is the secular equivalent of the biblical proverb. But the motto was doubtless understood by those who adopted it for the University in a spiritual, indeed a Christian sense, given the Christian foundation of the University. What, then, can we say about its spiritual significance?

It is, of course, a statement taken from the Hebrew Scriptures, the earlier Testament of what became the Christian Bible. There it occurs some four times. It stands fitly at the beginning of Proverbs (1:7) as a kind of superscription or summary of all that is to follow: "The fear of the LORD is the beginning of knowledge; fools despise wisdom and instruction." It stands again at the conclusion of the introductory section, this time with an addition that according to the general practice of Hebrew poetry adds a further sentiment to clarify it:[1] "The fear of the LORD is the beginning of wisdom, *and the knowledge of the Holy One is insight*" (Prov. 9:10). It is added as a conclusion to a Psalm which is manifestly a song of praise by a worshipper who shares his insights with a congregation: "The fear of the LORD is the beginning of wisdom; all those who practise it have a good understanding" (Ps. 111:10). And, finally, it comes again in a wisdom context in Job 28:28, where Job himself comments on how God alone knows the way to the wisdom that is hidden from mankind, "and he said to humankind, 'Truly, the fear of the Lord, that is wisdom; and to depart from evil is understanding.'"[2] There appears to be widespread agreement among scholars that the primary sense of the "fear of the LORD" is what we would nowadays call religion, a sense of reverence for God that affects people's lives in every area; it is not terror in the face of an arbitrary and capricious deity who continually threatens judgement on wrongdoers.

The sentiment remained alive in Judaism and we find it quoted and amplified in Sirach 1:14, 16, 18, 20 where the fear of the Lord is successively the "beginning, fullness, crown and root" of wisdom. In 19:20 it is "the whole of wisdom" (cf 21:11).[3]

Wisdom as God's gift in the New Testament

The proverb itself does not recur in the New Testament but the concepts that make it up are both present and it is interesting to see what happens to them.

The topic of wisdom has attracted much attention in New Testament study for a variety of reasons.[4] The most significant is that there are a number of passages where the kind of thing that is said about wisdom in the Old Testament and Judaism is also said about Jesus. In particular, wisdom is personified in a number of places and placed alongside God as his partner in creation and his rule over the world (Prov. 8:22-31; Wisdom 7:22 - 8:8). Wisdom is also equated with the law or Torah which is sent down from God to be with his people for their guidance and instruction (Sirach 24:1-12, 23). When we ask what influenced early Christian thinkers as they pondered how to express their understanding of Jesus, it seems clear that the Jewish language about wisdom was taken over and applied to Jesus (cf Heb. 1:3 and Wisdom 7:25f). "Wisdom christology" has become a major industry in recent years. And there is the fascinating question as to whether Jesus himself claimed any relationship with wisdom. Was he perhaps an envoy of wisdom? Or did he claim some kind of identity with wisdom?[5]

The interest of the debate is heightened by the fact that in second-century Gnosticism we come across Wisdom as a personified female figure - reflecting the facts that *hokhmah* and *sophia* are feminine nouns and that already in Proverbs Wisdom is a female figure. People looking for a female principle in

God have read back the kind of personification found in Gnosticism into first-century Christianity and linked together the Holy Spirit (a neuter noun in Greek) and Wisdom.

These tantalising hints are all that space permits us here. Our present concern is rather with the undeniable importance of wisdom as a Christian quality. Granted that there is a certain reaction against human, worldly wisdom (2 Cor. 1:12) which can be mere cleverness and give rise to pride and arrogance (1 Cor. 1:17ff) or which is expressed in splendid, but empty rhetoric (1 Cor. 2:1-5) and which is ultimately foolishness (1 Cor. 3:18f; cf 2 Pet. 1:16 of mythology), there is nevertheless a stress on the wisdom which is God's gift to his people. Jesus promises wisdom of speech to his followers when they have to testify for him (Luke 21:15), and the promise is fulfilled for the Christian witness Stephen (Acts 6:3, 10). And the promise is generalised to extend to Christian believers (Rom. 16:19; Eph. 1:17; 5:15; Col. 1:9, 28; 3:16; 4:5; Jas. 1:5; 3:13, 17; cf. 2 Tim. 3:15). Wisdom is associated with knowledge gained by revelation (1 Cor. 2:7, 13; Eph. 1:17; Col. 1:9) and communicated by people endowed with the Spirit (1 Cor. 12:8).

But the content of this Christian wisdom is not made clear. It is associated with the teaching about Christ (Col. 3:16). The Old Testament equation with the fear of the Lord is not repeated. It would seem that the New Testament goes a different route from the Old Testament in that it conceives of wisdom more as revelation given by God than as "the wise thing for people to do if they want to live as God's people".

Fear in the Christian life?
Nevertheless, the other side of the equation also takes on a life of its own. Particularly in Acts we come across the designation "those who fear God" for Gentiles who were attracted to the Jewish religion but had not taken the step of circumcision (Acts 13:16, 26).[6] Here the phrase has become a technical term, but a meaningful one. When Cornelius in particular is described in these terms (Acts 10:2, 22), it is plain that his was a practising religion that expressed itself in concern for other people as well as in prayers. But the appearance of the same phrase in Mary's

Song shows that this was a standard description of godly people in Old Testament language (Luke 1:50). A less positive content is seen in the words of the unjust judge who confessed that he did not fear God (Luke 18:4, cf 2) and in the comment of the penitent thief to his fellow "Do you not fear God?" (Luke 23:40); here the thought is more on the level of the dread that wrongdoers should feel and that should restrain them from evil acts.

In the teaching of Jesus we have the warning to people not to fear men as those who can kill the body but rather to fear God who can cast people into Gehenna (Luke 12:4f par. Matt. 10:26-28). Here the point is clearly a call to courage in the face of persecution for one's faith using the argument that apostasy leads to something more fearful than the death of the body. Alongside this saying, we should place others where fear of men is condemned precisely because God is on the side of his people and will protect and help them. This thought is expressed most clearly in Heb. 13:6, citing Ps. 118:6, but it is also present in the verses immediately following the Lucan saying: "do not fear; you are worth more than many sparrows" (Luke 12:6f). So the point is not a simple "don't fear men, lest something more fearful still may happen to you". The warning is a general one to all people (including those who kill other people's bodies) that they cannot escape the judgement of God, but side by side with it is the reassurance to God's people that they need not be afraid of what will happen to them. Other passages will demonstrate that they need not be afraid of God himself.

It is impossible to avoid this sense that God as judge is to be feared by wrongdoers. The condition of evil people is summed up in Rom. 3.18 as "there is no fear of God before their eyes"; their mental horizon does not include the fact of God and fear of him. To put it in this form may sound harsh to the modern ear. If we said "they have no respect for right and wrong", we should have preserved one aspect of the saying. But we should have lost the other aspect which is in effect to say "people who have no respect for right and wrong should be afraid of the consequences of their attitude". Within human societies systems of law and order endeavour to make it their aim that people will respect the law because they know that they will suffer penalties if they do not do so. It is difficult to see how this element of fear can be excluded from the motivation of people at large to keep the laws. Our own self-consciousness tells us that, if laws were not attended by sanctions, we should break them much more often than we do. The often-voiced feeling that people should not be motivated by fear is surely delusory idealism. By nature we have a sensitivity to pain, and this acts as a necessary and even beneficent warning against doing ourselves harm; the person who touches a hot surface and feels pain instinctively withdraws from contact and makes a conscious effort to do so: the pain is a warning signal lest greater harm be done to the body. The person suffering from leprosy who loses the sensitivity of the nerve-endings on the skin is in great danger of suffering bodily damage. It is, therefore, not easy to see why the fear of pain should not be a legitimate motive on the moral level also. Fear of the Judge prevents us from doing things which will harm ourselves.

The intent of sayings such as those of Jesus, therefore, is not to create an impression of God as a tyrant who enjoys punishing people but rather to appeal to people's good sense not to act in ways that are evil and will bring harm upon them.

To be sure, sayings that speak about doing certain things "with fear and trembling" (1 Cor. 2:3; 2 Cor. 7:15; Eph. 6:5; Phil. 2:12) strike a strange chord in modern ears. But I wonder if one of the shortcomings of modern society is not a certain flippancy and refusal to take things seriously. The solemn language of marriage vows in church is hardly taken seriously by people who within a few years find themselves seeking divorce, and the lack of real commitment reflected in the growing practice of cohabitation without tying the bond tightly and permanently points in the same direction. Laws and customs are increasingly seen as human arrangements with no ultimate basis, and you keep them only if you want to or are prevented by sanctions from doing otherwise.

"Fear not"

At the same time, we have the many sayings which command people not to be afraid of God or of his messengers. The instinctive reaction to a theophany or an angelic visitor in the Old Testament is terror, and the response of the heavenly being is generally introduced by "Do not be afraid", since the purpose of the visitation is beneficial. So too in the New Testament there are numerous examples of encouragements not to be afraid of heavenly figures (Luke 1:13, 30; 2:10), and when Jesus appears as a heavenly or numinous figure he uses the same formula (Mark 6:50; Luke 5:10).

The next step is when people are told that the proper attitude of believers is not to fear in relation to God or anybody else. Believers have received the position of sons or children of God with the implication that this is not a situation where one fears God (Rom. 8:15). This saying stands in tension with that in 1 Pet. 1:17 where believers are to fear the God who is both their Father and their impartial judge. The point here, of course, is that people are not to take advantage of their position as God's children to think that he is partial towards them and will not punish them for wrongdoing, the kind of attitude that comes to light in Wisdom 12:22 - although that text must be put into a context of God also being strict towards his people and more lenient to their enemies to give them opportunity for repentance (Wisdom 12:20f).

The ultimate hope is for a situation in which love is supreme and dispossesses fear from believers (1 John 4:18). Here the ideal is a situation in which people so love and obey God that they have no need to fear him.

We thus have a paradox of the Christian life before us in that fear of the Lord is upheld as the characteristic attitude of the Christian, but at the same time the Christian is to love God in a relationship in which fear has no place. Insofar as we are sinners, we are to fear the Lord, but insofar as we are his children, we are to love him. The New Testament is realistic in recognising that we remain sinful or in danger of falling into sin.

Fear and godliness
The result of our discussion is that fear of God is not seen as entirely negative. It is regarded positively as a description of true religion.

This becomes further evident when we turn, finally, into the Pastoral Epistles.[7] Here we encounter the term *eusebeia* and its cognates (together with *theosebeia*), which is generally translated as "godliness" or "piety". It is a term which has often been thought to represent the taking over of a Greek ideal into biblical religion, the concept of respect for God and the orders of creation, and therefore to some extent a secularisation, if not actual degeneration, of biblical religion into the kind of attitude typical of better-quality pagan society. However, investigation shows that the term was already at home among Greek-speaking Jews, and that among them it represented the phrase "fear of the Lord" (cf the juxtaposition in Acts 10:2). Here, then, we have a shift in translation which brings out the element of dutiful respect to God and plays down the element of actual "fear". Hence the word can be used in the Pastoral Epistles especially to signify the whole of Christian behaviour; it stands alongside faith as an all-encompassing term for the Christian life (1 Tim. 2:2; 4:7f; 6:3, 5f, 11; 2 Tim. 3:5; Titus 1:1) and indeed for the Christian religion (1 Tim. 3:16).

The importance of this shift, which took place in Judaism and was inherited by some branches of Christianity, is that it demonstrates the capacity of Judaism and Christianity to develop new terminology and new conceptuality. It is partly a matter of developing a vocabulary that will speak in a new situation, that will make traditional ideas meaningful. It is also a case of development in understanding, so that specific ideas get appropriate emphasis.

At the same time, we in our generation have to beware of assuming that we can move forwards and abandon the concepts associated with "fear" of the Lord, and consign them to the theology of the past. This is readily apparent within the Pastoral Epistles where the use of the term "fear" is not entirely abandoned (1 Tim. 5:20). Even in 1 John with its teaching about not fearing God the possibility of living in the darkness and shrinking away in shame before Christ at his *parousia* is clearly depicted (1 John 2:9, 28).

The motto of the University, then, is not stated in the New Testament as it is in the Old. Both parts of it, however, have an on-going life of their own, the concept of wisdom being focussed on the person of Jesus as the embodiment of God's saving purpose for his creation and developing more and more into the revelation of that purpose; and the concept of fear expressing that serious-minded respect for God and his laws which must stand alongside the deep and joyful relationship of love which his people have with him. Such a motto may seem very distant from the secular life of a modern University; it remains the task of those who accept it as their guide for life to commend its truth by the quality of their living and the integrity of their testimony.

5

THE WISDOM OF GOD AND THE WISDOM OF THE WORLD THEOLOGY AND THE UNIVERSITY

Brian S Rosner

The University of Aberdeen, like other ancient universities, was created by the church. Consequently the study of theology has held a secure place among its academic offerings from the very beginning. However, five hundred years on with the secularisation of the university, which is now taken for granted, many would question whether theology can serve the university in the modern world. In this essay I would like to consider the reverse of this question, which, though less pressing, is no less important. It is this: Can the university serve theology? Several other questions make the issue clear: What are the potential dangers and benefits of studying and teaching theology in an academic setting? Must teachers of Christian theology necessarily be committed Christians (a condition which the university does not require)? What has the wisdom of the world to do with the wisdom of God? Our answers to these questions arise from reflections upon texts in 1 Corinthians, Romans and Colossians which deal with wisdom, the subject of the University motto.

The wisdom of God

The word wisdom occurs more often in 1 Corinthians 1-2 than any other place in the New Testament. Apparently the Corinthian Christians were judging Paul (see 4:1-5) by the standards of the Greek philosophical or sophistic tradition, with its emphasis on rhetorical skill and human understanding. On this score Paul had been found wanting. They were enamoured by "the wisdom of this world" which was taught by "the wise, the scribes and the debaters of this age" (1:20). As Professor Robin Barbour, Professor of New Testament at Aberdeen from 1972 to 1982, commented in his article 'Wisdom and the Cross in 1 Corinthians 1 and 2': "It may be taken for granted that he [Paul] is influenced [in his use of 'wisdom'] by the Corinthians' use of the term."[1]

Corinth was a proud intellectual centre in Paul's day with a steady stream of travelling lecturers who charged fees to the public to attend their extra-mural programmes. They operated a kind of mobile Open University. In effect, the Corinthians were impressed by what could be called the ancient equivalent of the modern university. If we allow this identification, 1 Corinthians 1-2 may be read for Paul's assessment of the place of the university in the task of theology. At the risk of understatement, it is not a very positive assessment.

In 1:18-25 Paul argues that the gospel is a contradiction to human wisdom. The best human intellects did not arrive at God's scheme of redemption, a crucified messiah. "The world did not come to know God through wisdom" (1:21). As Professor Barbour has noted (p. 63): "it is clear that the total unexpectedness of God's act of salvation in the cross has ... made foolish or cancelled out all 'man-made' worldly wisdom on the subject of salvation or redemption." In fact God's way was designed to outsmart the wise (1:19). God's disregard for human standards of wisdom, is, Paul says, clearly seen in the composition of the congregation in Corinth itself: God chose 'nobodies' to make up the new people of God, not the powerful, noble and wise (1:26-31). Paul himself shunned the clever and impressive approach of the sophists when he arrived in Corinth, preferring instead to come in weakness so that the faith of the Corinthian believers might be in God alone and not in his eloquence and persuasive oratory (2:1-5). Climactically and conclusively, in 2:6-16 Paul explains that God's wisdom, the stuff of theology, can only be received with the aid of the Spirit. The person without the Spirit "is not able to understand" (2:14), just as a deaf person usually cannot appreciate music. Paul stresses the limits of the human intellect, the stuff of the university, when it comes to theology, which concerns the knowledge of God. Whereas the university is concerned with the pursuit of knowledge, knowledge of God is for Paul established in Christ through the gospel (2 Cor. 4:6). That is why Paul can say that Christ himself becomes the embodiment of wisdom for Christians (1 Cor. 1:31).

Such knowledge is inextricably linked to obedience and godliness, as can be seen from Paul's prayer in Colossians 1:9-10:

> "And so, from the day we heard of it [the conversion of the Colossians], we have not ceased to pray for you, asking that you might be filled with the knowledge of his will in all spiritual wisdom and understanding, to lead a life worthy of the Lord, fully pleasing to him, bearing fruit in every good work."

Knowledge of God here is not an end in itself. Its purpose is to produce a lifestyle which, Paul goes on to explain in chapters 3-4, is characterised by compassion, kindness, lowliness, meekness, patience and, above all, love towards other Christians, family members and outsiders.

The book of Romans, Paul's most overtly theological letter, reinforces the impression that the wisdom and knowledge of God carries weighty implications for life. Having explored a key subject of theology in Romans 9-11, the faithfulness of God to his promises to Israel, Paul concludes in 11:33-36 with a doxology, demonstrating that theology ought to lead to worship: "O the depths of the riches of the wisdom and knowledge of God! How unsearchable are his judgements and how inscrutable his ways!" (11:33).

According to Paul theology and doxology belong together. Undevotional theology (and untheological devotion, for that matter) is far from the ideal. If doxology without theology amounts to idolatry (praise without accurate thoughts about God is nothing more than idol worship), theology without doxology, which is what many universities might recommend, is seriously truncated. Such theology is like a rose bush without the roses (nothing but thorns and prickles - not worth the effort).

Romans 12-15, which follows on from Paul's exposition of the righteousness of God in the gospel in chapters 1-11, takes us a step further. Here Paul shows that theology must lead to obedience; doctrine combines with duty. In Romans 12:1-2 studying "the mercies of God" is supposed to lead to "presenting your body to God as a living sacrifice." "The renewed mind" is the basis for behavioural "transformation." Theology without practice is also somehow unnatural; it produces tadpoles instead of frogs - big heads (for thinking) without arms and legs (for action). In this light the discipline of Practical Theology ought not to be seen as a dispensable luxury nor as 'icing on the cake'. It is the goal to which all the other disciplines must lead. When rightly understood theology shapes all of life and is always practical.

For Paul God is not an appropriate object for cool, critical, detached, scientific observation and evaluation. He would not recommend a purely academic interest in God. Paul would consider it futile and hazardous to try to sever our personal theological commitments and discipleship from our academic work in theology. It is ironic that modern hermeneutical theory lends some support to Paul's view. It doubts not so much the advisability of such objectivity, but its very possibility. Each of us approaches biblical texts and theological questions with our own pre-understandings, opinions, values and world-view intact and these, however hard we try, cannot be totally circumvented.

Thus there are real dangers for those studying theology in a university. In such an environment the proper goals of theology can be missed completely and the whole exercise distorted.

The wisdom of the world

Can anything be said in defence of the place of the university in the enterprise of theology? In view of the dangers mentioned above, perhaps we should take the quincentenary as an opportunity to call it a day. In other words, have I argued myself out of a job?

The remarks of Paul that do most damage to the notion of an academic study of theology occur in 1 Corinthians 2:14:

> "The unspiritual man does not receive the gifts of the Spirit of God, for they are folly to him, and he is not able to understand them because they are spiritually discerned" (RSV).

The key problem for the interpretation of this verse for our purposes is whether the unbeliever is incapable of intellectually comprehending the wisdom of God or if the incapacity lies rather in the area of personal appraisal and reception. Upon closer inspection the latter turns out to be the more accurate reading of the text. The verb translated "understand" is literally "to know", which throughout 1 Corinthians 1-2 has to do with knowing something (or someone) personally and intimately and not just with intellectual knowledge. It is not that "the natural man" cannot understand or explain God's truth. Without the Spirit's work he or she cannot appreciate the gospel (it appears foolish) and thus will not respond positively to it.

The notion of "spiritual discernment" in 2:14b makes clear what is at stake. The term in question concerns examination and enquiry leading to an assessment. In places like Athens it was sometimes used in legal contexts. It occurs ten times in 1 Corinthians, but nowhere else in Paul's letters. On every occasion, except in 14:24, Paul uses it polemically or ironically, which suggests that it was a favourite word of some 'educated' Corinthian Christians who flattered themselves as being "discerning" and therefore superior. Paul's response to this attitude is devastating: he asserts that it is possession of the Spirit, not human wisdom, that makes one "discerning." However, Paul is not saying that those without the Spirit cannot understand the things of the Spirit. Rather, such people are not able to make appropriate judgements about God and His work in the world. Romans 8:5 is a kindred thought that helps explain Paul's point: "those who live according to the flesh set their minds on the things of the flesh; but those who live according to the Spirit set their minds on the things of the Spirit"[2]. The issue is one of appreciation rather than cognition. Although not ideal, it is perfectly possible to teach Christian theology without having a faith commitment.

Christian faith is not gnosticism, in which a secret knowledge is only available to the initiated. People are saved in the Christian faith not by some secret knowledge, but by responding to knowledge that is proclaimed publicly and available to all without distinction.

It is not just in Christian theology that there is a debate as to the appropriateness of those not committed to the faith explaining the religious texts of that faith. Jews have for a long time complained about the failure of many Christian scholars to understand properly their religious literature. Although the debate continues, there is something to be said for the view that the interpreter of a religious document should ideally have at least some sympathy for the teaching he or she expounds. The sectarian literature of the Dead Sea Scrolls, which is no longer the religious literature of any group, demonstrates the impossibility of insisting on any more than this in the broad area of the study of religion. There are no Qumran sectaries available to perform the job!

On the other hand, the diversity of interpreters that a university setting supplies, in the absence of confessional standards, can have its benefits. Since the task of interpretation is by definition in part subjective, having participants from different backgrounds and faiths (and even 'non-faiths') can be enriching. A different vantage point often brings different questions to the task and observations are made of data that would otherwise go unnoticed.

Many of the skills and disciplines involved in studying theology do not in fact presuppose faith. In biblical studies alone, due to the huge cultural gap between our day and biblical times, a host of university disciplines play a critical role. These include Linguistics, Geography, Archaeology, Ancient History, Sociology, Literary Studies and Philosophy. To take another example, Practical Theology brings together the study of Psychology, Politics, Biology, Ecology, Communication, Education, Ethics ... the potential list is endless.

Theological study at the most serious level is a veritable intellectual melting pot to an extent that is arguably not true of any other subject in the university. Since this is the case, it is necessary for theology to be studied in the most rigorous fashion, paying more than simply lip service to these other disciplines, if it is to maintain credibility and avoid serious decline. A university makes this possible, at least in theory.

Along with and balancing Paul's stress on the importance of the illumination of the Spirit is his high regard for the place of the mind in general. Paul nowhere gives the impression that Christians are to stop thinking. Indeed there is nothing in the Pauline corpus that would support an irrational approach to faith or an anti-intellectualism. For Paul the work of the Spirit is not in opposition to the mind, as in some forms of Greek philosophy and religion in his day. For example, in 1 Corinthians 14:19-

20 Paul prefers the full use of the mind to ecstatic experience in corporate worship:

> "in church I would rather speak five words with my mind, in order to instruct others, than ten thousand words in a tongue. Brothers and sisters, do not be children in your thinking; be babes in evil, but in thinking be mature" (cf 1 Cor. 14:14-15).

Like any university Paul values intelligible words and clear thoughts. He also puts a premium on teaching and instruction, both in the home (Eph. 6:4; cf Deut. 6:6-7) and in the church (Col. 3:16: "teach and admonish one another in all wisdom"). Christian proclamation for Paul is not only about "preaching", but includes the rational processes of "defence", "argument" and "persuasion" (2 Cor. 5:11; Phil. 1:7; Acts 17:2ff; 19:8). Paul, it appears, takes for granted the notion he received from his Jewish inheritance that study can be a true expression of devotion to God. The basic message of the Jewish tractate Aboth, to take a prominent early example, is the idea that the study of Torah is our highest joy and the reason for our existence. Torah-study, even in its most painstaking and rigorous form, is a type of worship. Jews have generally held on to this high view of intellectual pursuits (producing more than their share of Nobel Prize winners). This high view of the mind is a notion that is based upon the doctrine of creation itself: as rational beings we are created in the image of God.

While it is true that in Paul's letters it is taught that the thinking, reasoning and reflective aspect of human consciousness, which we call the mind, can suffer corruption (Rom. 1:28; Col. 2:18; 1 Tim. 6:5), it can also be redeemed and renewed (Rom. 12:2). That the mind can be a positive thing for Christians is seen most clearly in Paul's affirmation: "we have the mind of Christ" (1 Cor. 2:16; cf Phil. 2:5).

Can the university serve theology? The dangers of studying and teaching theology in an academic setting are not to be underestimated. Nonetheless, the opportunities for the interdisciplinary work it affords and the high standards it demands should also not be ignored as genuine benefits.

6

STUDY ROOTED IN DEVOTION - THE
ABERDEEN THEOLOGICAL TRADITION

Ian Bradley

One of the most striking features in the corporate life of the
Department of Divinity with Religious Studies at Aberdeen
University is the brief period of Bible reading and prayer which
ends the daily mid-morning coffee break held in the Chaplaincy.
Some students find it an inappropriate intrusion of Christian
devotion into the life of an institution committed to the academic study of religion rather than the propagation of one particular faith. While there is certainly room for debate about its
continuing appropriateness today, the custom of daily prayer
and the weekly Chapter Service of Holy Communion in King's
College Chapel stand in a long and distinctive Aberdeen tradition of rooting theological study in prayer and devotion, at both
a personal and corporate level.

There is, indeed, a strong case to be made for identifying
this tradition as the distinguishing feature of theological education at Aberdeen. If one were to embark on the invidious and
risky exercise of ranking the four Divinity Faculties of Scotland
according to their contribution to various strands of Christian
life and thought through the centuries, then Aberdeen would
surely come at the top of the 'spirituality' league. Edinburgh
and St Andrews have almost certainly produced greater and more
disputatious theologians, Glasgow more recruits for the parish
and mission field. Aberdeen's special strength has lain in the
less tangible but no less important field of personal devotion
and the promotion and improvement of public worship, It is,
perhaps, not too much to say that while the particular contribution to the church as a whole of Edinburgh and St Andrews has
been theological, and Glasgow's practical and pastoral, then
Aberdeen's has been devotional and liturgical.

If the University's motto encapsulates the idea that intellectual activity should always be grounded in a sense of fear and

wonder in the face of the awesome mystery of God, the character of the founder exemplifies the principle of *lex credendi, lex orandi* which has been at the heart of the Aberdeen approach to theology. William Elphinstone was first and foremost a churchman, deeply committed to the worship of God. It is significant that the achievement which stands second only to the founding of Aberdeen University among his life's works should lie in the field of liturgy. The *Aberdeen Breviary*, which he compiled and published in 1510, was an early attempt to provide a distinctively Scottish service book in the Medieval Catholic Church. An adaptation of the *Sarum Breviary*, it introduced hymns, antiphons, collects and lessons for services commemorating the Celtic Saints in Scotland and did much to revive worship in the period before the Reformation.

Elphinstone was very clear that the University which he founded in 1495 should be a place of worship as well as of academic excellence. By the time of his death in 1514, and as a result of his endowments, there were, in fact, more chaplains on the establishment (eight) than teachers (six) as well as six choir boys. The principle of close integration between study and devotion which he laid down was not lost in the Reformation. It is true that the prebendary chaplains and the choir boys went but worship remained a very important part of the life of King's College. Students were expected to attend public worship at St Machar's Cathedral where they would hear the Principal preach in his capacity as parish minister. The so-called New Foundation, promulgated between 1587 and 1593, also laid down detailed regulations for religious instruction on the Sabbath.

How far this rigorous regime, with its considerable demands on teachers and students alike, was actually put into practice we do not know. Certainly life at King's became slack in the early seventeenth century, The man who brought it round again, Patrick Forbes, Bishop of Aberdeen, 1618-35 was a figure of deep piety who stands very clearly in the Aberdeen tradition of theology rooted in devotion.

Forbes was both mentor and role model for that important and sadly neglected group of seventeenth century divines known as the Aberdeen Doctors. The six men who stood out against the Covenanters and tried desperately to prevent the fissure between Episcopalianism and Presbyterianism included three leading Aberdeen academics: Patrick Forbes' son, John, who held the Chair of Divinity at King's College from 1620 to 1641; William Leslie, Principal of King's College from 1630 to 1639, and Robert Baron, Professor of Divinity at Marischal College from 1625. It was because of their dislike of theological factiousness and disputation, their eirenic vision of a broad church which could embrace differing ideas about church order and liturgy and their strong sense that matters of ecclesiastical government and administration were of secondary importance to the worship of God, the care of souls and the fostering of the devotional life that the Aberdeen Doctors took on the hyper-Calvinistic Covenanters.

Although they were ultimately unsuccessful in their attempt to counter the Covenanters' narrow dogmatism, the broader vision of the church which characterised the outlook of the Aberdeen Doctors was not lost. Their particular concerns, the reconciling of Presbyterians and Episcopalians, the importance of formal liturgy in worship and the need to root the life of the church in prayer and devotion rather than theological dispute, have resurfaced again and again over the last 350 years, not least among their successors in Aberdeen. The spiritual power of their writings is also considerable although, even in our own age of revived interest in spirituality and devotion, it is still largely waiting to be rediscovered. Who now reads the *Spiritual Exercises* of John Forbes, noted down between 1624 and 1647, which are part diary and part meditation and explore the mystical communion between humans and God based on the importance of the Eucharist?

In one of the few recent published studies of the Aberdeen Doctors, the Anglican scholar AM Allchin has pointed to the remarkable spiritual content of sermons delivered by James Sibbald, minister of St Nicholas Church from 1625 until 1639 when he was ejected from his pulpit and elected Dean of the Faculty of Theology at King's College. The sermons, which were published in 1658 a decade after his death in exile in Dublin, have as their theme the duty which is laid on all Christians to worship God and the joy they find there, especially through participation in the Eucharist:

> "The proper sacrifice of Christians is the sacrifice of praise and thanksgiving, everywhere vehemently urged in the New Testament. Our blessed Lord did institute the blessed sacrament of his body and blood giving thanks, and for this end that we may give thanks to God, as for all his benefits, so especially for that of redemption. By the right performance of this duty, we begin our heaven on earth, for the proper exercise of heaven is praise."[1]

Sibbald had a great sense of the reciprocal nature of the human encounter with God which takes place in worship. He portrays God drawing us to him through his grace and love and our responding by moving towards him. As Allchin points out, he was unusually attracted to the doctrine of *theosis*, found among certain mystics and commonly in the Eastern tradition but largely neglected by both Catholics and Protestants in the West. He saw the natural destiny of humans as being to grow in holiness and eventually become one with God. In this process of deification both personal devotion and public worship, seen as a sacrifice of praise and thanksgiving, play a very important part. This leads Sibbald to have a very high conception of the priestly function of the ordained ministry while still holding strongly to the Reformation principle of the priesthood of all believers.

The strong spirituality of the Aberdeen doctors must have enhanced the atmosphere of King's College in the 1620s and 1630s as a place of godliness as well as of good learning. Laws promulgated in the 1640s suggest there may have been a slippage in devotional observances after their departure. Punishments were prescribed for those absent from morning and evening prayers, an understandable offence when morning prayers accompanied by a sermon were held at 6.30 a.m. in the winter and 6 a.m. in the spring and summer terms. Between dinner and supper every evening the bursars were required to read, on a rota system, portions of the Old and New Testaments. Students were enjoined to pray alone in their rooms every evening at 9 o'clock after reading a chapter of the Bible. Junior students were to have the aid of appointed liturgical forms and orders to help them in this task.

The regulations surviving from this period also point to communal singing of the Psalms by students every night in King's College. Aberdeen can, in fact, claim an important place in the history of Scottish metrical psalmody. The *sang schule* established in the late Middle Ages to train boys and clergy survived the Reformation to become one of the most important centres of church music in late sixteenth and seventeenth century Scotland. Andrew Kemp, master of the Aberdeen song school from 1570-73, produced forty settings of psalm tunes. In 1625 Edward Raban, an English printer whom Patrick Forbes had brought to Aberdeen after periods in Edinburgh and St Andrews, produced the first Scottish psalter to publish psalm tunes with harmonies. It was this psalter which introduced the popular tune 'Bon-Accord', sung in reports (i.e. with phrases being taken up and repeated by different voices).

The second half of the seventeenth century saw King's College nurture three of the most important figures in the Aberdeen tradition of theology rooted in devotion. Henry Scougal(1650-78) entered the college at the age of fifteen, was made a tutor at nineteen and was Professor of Divinity from 1674 until his untimely death four years later. His *Life of God in the Soul of Man* is rightly regarded as one of the devotional classics of the seventeenth century and must count as one of the treasures of Scottish spirituality. In it, Scougal defined true religion as "a union of the soul with God, a real participation in the divine nature, the very image of God drawn upon the soul".[2] His call for Christians to grow in holiness, which echoes Sibbald's doctrine of *theosis*, had an enormous impact on John Wesley. It has even been suggested that the Holy Club founded by Wesley and his friends in Oxford in the 1730s which gave rise to the Methodist movement may have been based on a similar group formed in Aberdeen some sixty years earlier. Like the Aberdeen Doctors Scougal put both private and personal devotion at the centre of the Christian life. The way towards 'begetting a holy and religious disposition by faith', he suggested, was through 'fervent and hearty prayer' and 'frequent and conscientious use' of the sacrament of the Lord's Supper.[3]

The same sense of prayerfulness characterised the life and writings of two brothers, James and George Garden, both of whom read Divinity at King's College in the late 1660s. James (1645-1726) was Professor of Divinity at King's from 1681 until 1697 when he was ejected from his chair for refusing to take the oath of allegiance to William and Mary. A staunch Episcopalian and Jacobite, he became a follower of the French Roman Catholic mystics, Mesdames Bourignon and Guyon. Disliking the hair-splitting dogmatism of Presbyterianism, his stress on worship rather than preaching and lecturing drew him more and more away from the established Church of Scotland. His *Comparative Theology* was written to emphasise the devotional element in theology as against the dogmatic.

James' younger brother George (1649-1733) served as minister of St Machar's Cathedral from 1679 and St Nicholas Church, Aberdeen from 1683. In 1692 he, too, was deprived of his charge by the Privy Council for refusing to pray for William II and Mary and maintaining loyalty to the Jacobite cause. He spent most of the remainder of his life living quietly in Aberdeen ministering to a small Episcopalian congregation which met in an oratory in his house. Like his elder brother, George Garden also developed close links with French Roman Catholic mystics. In 1709 and 1710 Garden wrote two long letters to a friend in Fife on the subject of contemplative prayer which are remarkable for their spiritual sensitivity and depth. Garden advocated "silent prayer and pure faith in God". He was emphatic that prayer was not a matter of technique but rather of attitude - "an entire resignation of your own will, opinions, reason, affections, and all unto God":

> "The prayer of silence being the soul's turning away the understanding from all the creatures and all their images and the fixing it by pure faith on God the supreme truth and good, as he is in himself infinitely beyond the conceptions of any creature, and by ardently loving that supreme and boundless and incomprehensible loveliness, the great end of this is to be rooted and grounded in divine hope and love, and in all virtue."[4]

There is no easy route to deep spiritual experiences, little consolation even, in Garden's writings on contemplative prayer. Rather he shares with the great Spanish mystic, St John of the Cross, a sense of 'The Dark Night of the Soul'. All we can do is proceed as if we were blind, moving by faith rather than by sight, trusting not our own eyes, not even the divine light within us, but submitting to the grace and guidance of God.

> "The soul is placed in a dry and thirsty land where no water is: and yet it does still more hunger and thirst after God and prayer, and its disgust of temporal things increases the more, while it seems to itself to have no virtue and not to love God. And this is its true purification, not merely from the images, and the love of bodily things, but from self, self-love, self-complacency, self-seeking, or the cleaving to anything but God."[5]

During the nineteenth century another important element in the Aberdeen tradition of theology rooted in personal devotion comes into focus with the key role of King's College in nurturing the distinctive Gaelic spirituality of Highland Evangelicalism. Three of the greatest Gaelic preachers of the period received their training here in the early years of the century: John MacDonald (1779-1849), successively minister of Culloden and Ferintosh and known as 'The Apostle of the North', Alexander MacLeod (1786-1869), 'Great Alexander of the Gospel', who served in Uig (Lewis), Lochalsh and Rogart, and John MacRae (1794-1876), whose charges included Cross (Lewis), Knockbain and Greenock. The influence of Aberdeen on these men, and the many others who followed them, has yet to be studied but it surely helped to deepen and mould their distinctive Highland and island spirituality.

The latter part of the nineteenth century saw a conscious return to several of the themes pursued by the Aberdeen Doctors and particularly to the central importance of worship in the life of the church. The key figure here was William Milligan, Professor of Biblical Criticism at King's College from 1850 to 1875. Feeling that the eternal priesthood of Christ had been greatly neglected in Scotland, he sought to re-emphasise it in the context of a reformed understanding of the priesthood of all believers by stressing the importance of the Eucharist and arguing for its weekly celebration.

Milligan was a seminal influence on the so-called Scoto-Catholic movement which did so much to revive the liturgical practice of the Church of Scotland in the second half of the nineteenth century. He was one of the founders of the Scottish Church Society in 1892 and became its first president. Perhaps his most devoted pupil and disciple was James Cooper who studied under him at King's before taking up his first charge in Broughty Ferry and then returning to Aberdeen in 1881 as minister of the East Church of St Nicholas. In 1886 Cooper founded the Aberdeen Ecclesiological Society, the first of its kind in Scotland, to study the principles of church architecture and promote a more liturgical style of church building and furnishing. It was thanks to the efforts of this and similar societies that Presbyterian churches in Scotland came to be built with side-pulpits, lecterns and prayer desks.

At the end of the nineteenth century in King's College, student participation in public worship was still regarded as being just as important as attendance at lectures. From 1843 the Free Church College at the other end of the city also expected regular attendance at divine service from its students. Christ's College brought its own important contribution to the Aberdeen tradition of rooting theological study in the context of private and corporate worship, introducing a weekly Divinity chapter service, instituted by Professor GD Henderson, then Master of the College, and regular student retreats at the Burn and Angus House in Edzell.

A distinguished clutch of more recent graduates witness to the vigorous continuation of the tradition through the twentieth century. Martin Reith, who studied at King's in the 1930s and died in 1992, did much to rediscover and rehabilitate the distinctive spirituality of northern Scotland and himself felt called to lead the austere and solitary life of a Celtic hermit. David Ogston, minister of St John's Kirk in Perth, is one of the most innovative and creative liturgists in the contemporary Church of Scotland, drawing on the Eastern Orthodox tradition, Celtic Christianity and the riches of the Scots language to produce services characterised by colour, movement and vigour. David Strachan is a particularly sensitive interpreter of public worship for television and has deservedly won awards for several of his broadcast services. Ian White has developed a remarkable musical ministry based on his contemporary versions of the Psalms. There are doubtless many others whose liturgical talents or personal spirituality are unsung yet deeply appreciated by those around them.

What are the reasons for this particular tradition which I have tried to identify and discern in this short essay and which, I hope without too much special pleading, I have suggested can be claimed in a special way as Aberdeen's own? The strength of Episcopalianism in the north east is obviously a significant factor but it is not in itself enough to account for the particular strength of mysticism in the region described in GD Henderson's celebrated study for the Spalding Club in 1934.[6] Another important element may well have been Aberdeen's close proximity to and involvement with the distinctive religious culture of the Highlands and Islands with their own traditions of deep evangelical spirituality reaching back to the age of Celtic Christianity and fanned by more recent revivals. Perhaps, too, its relative geographical isolation has been important in enabling Aberdeen to keep its distance from the controversies consuming so much energy further south and to maintain its gentle and eirenic spirit. As the ancient Gaels demonstrated, there is much to be said for living out one's Christian faith on the margins rather than near the centre of society. Such, after all, was the position of Our Lord himself.

It is, I think, significant that so many of the great works which have come out of King's College over the last 500 years belong to the Chapel or the oratory rather than the classroom or the study: Elphinstone's *Breviary*, Raban's *Psalter*, Forbes' spiritual exercises, Sibbald's sermons, Scougal's meditations, Garden's letters and the liturgical interests of Milligan and Cooper. The Aberdeen way of doing theology has been to root it in worship and devotion. It has also been, with certain notable exceptions, to shun controversy and dispute. There has been a deeply eirenic strain, a strong ecumenical strain and also a clear evangelical strain. At its heart there has been a sense that the University, and particularly that part of it which is engaged in the study of Divinity, is a faith community as well as an intellectual community. There has been an understanding that new discoveries and personal growth are to be found in the chapel as much as in the classroom - that the spiritual dimension matters as much as the intellectual and the communal as much as the individual. At a time of growing pressure and growing secularism, this understanding must not be lost. That is why the current embodiment of the Aberdeen tradition in the daily Bible reading and prayers after coffee and at the weekly Chapter Communion service is so important.

7

THOMAS REID ON THE OBJECTIVITY OF MORALS

David Fergusson

In a recent lecture the Chief Rabbi, Jonathan Sacks, complains about our collective failure to acknowledge moral truths which are vital to the way we live as human beings.

> "We no longer believe in an objective moral order. Indeed, we think of the good as something to be pursued individually rather than sought collectively. Education is no longer seen as the induction of the young into the rules and virtues of society. Instead it has become a way of helping individuals make private choices as individuals. Above all, we are in danger of witnessing the end of the family as a stable and persisting unit through which future generations are nurtured, and through which we internalise the rules we have so painfully arrived at on our collective journey through history."[1]

Sacks' appeal for recognition of "an objective moral order" is presented not as a partisan political position of the right or the left but simply as a matter of social ecology. If our children are not raised to recognise the authority of moral demands "who can blame them if they translate the relativities of our ethics into the proposition that what is right is what I feel like doing and can get away with?"[2]

Yet it is one thing to inveigh against the corrosive tendencies of moral relativism but quite another to provide a credible account of moral realism, the view that moral truths are not of our own making but are in some sense given and thus await our discovery. In current philosophical debate we find powerful arguments on both sides. For the non-realist, moral values are to be construed as of our own making for the following reasons: i) historical accounts of moral diversity and change are best explained in terms of cultural context and human goals; ii) the notion of "objective" moral value or truth is metaphysically odd and cannot be satisfactorily elucidated; iii) the close connection between moral evaluation and action is more easily understood by a theory which explains morality by its relation to human desires and interests. It is the combination of these arguments which leads a contemporary philosopher like JL Mackie to conclude that morality is merely a human construct designed for the regulation of social conduct.[3] On the other hand, for the realist who believes that moral evaluation is more a matter of perceiving truths which we in no way invent, the following considerations will generally appear overriding: i) in moral judgement we regard ourselves as doing something other than expressing personal or social preferences; ii) the familiar phenomena of moral disagreement and conversion suggest that there is some fact of the matter at stake in the evaluations we make; iii) the importance of moral training is to be understood in terms of enabling people to perceive the world in a morally appropriate way - this training may be likened to that required for proper aesthetic perception.

It may seem surprising to invoke the work of an eighteenth century cleric and philosopher for guidance on this topic yet the work of Thomas Reid remains the subject of sustained scholarly interest. Reid was born into the manse of Strachan, Kincardineshire in 1710 and at the age of 12 he matriculated at Marischal College in Aberdeen.[4] After several years' work as librarian at Marischal he was presented by the professors at the rival institution of King's College to the pastoral charge of New Machar, about ten miles to the north west of Aberdeen. Reid served as the minister of New Machar from 1737-51 when he was persuaded to return to Aberdeen as a Regent at King's College. There he was a founder member of the distinguished Aberdeen Philosophical Society which is said to have met regularly in the Lion Inn on the Spital Hill near Reid's manse. Several papers that were delivered to the Philosophical Society adumbrated his *Inquiry into the Human Mind on the Principles of Common Sense* (1764). In the same year of publication Reid was appointed to succeed Adam Smith and Francis Hutcheson in the Chair of Moral Philosophy in the University of Glasgow. The remainder of his life was spent in Glasgow, and in retirement he published his two other major works, *Essays on the*

Intellectual Powers of Man (1785) and the *Essays on the Active Powers of Man* (1788). Reid's long life was in personal terms unremarkable. If as a preacher and lecturer he was not noted for his eloquence or oratorical skills he appears to have been regarded with affection as a pastor both by his parishioners in New Machar and his students in Aberdeen and Glasgow. His private life was marked by over 50 years of happy marriage to his cousin Elizabeth Reid although this was overshadowed by the death in their own lifetime of eight of nine sons and daughters. As a philosopher Reid's name is almost synonymous with the Scottish School of Common Sense Philosophy. His work was primarily reactive in significance as it sought to provide an adequate response to David Hume's scepticism. Reid wrote to Hume in 1763 from Aberdeen:

> "A little philosophical society here, ... is much indebted to you for its entertainment. Your company, although we are all good Christians, would be more acceptable than that of Athanasius; and since we cannot have you upon the bench, you are brought oftener than any other man to the bar; accused and defended with great zeal, but without bitterness. If you write no more in morals, politics, and metaphysics, I am afraid we shall be at a loss for subjects."[5]

Hume proved capable of a similarly gracious and characteristically charitable response:

> "I shall only say that if you have been able to clear up these abstruse and important subjects, instead of being mortified, I shall be so vain as to pretend to a share of the praise; and shall think that my errors, by having at least some coherence, have led you to make a more strict review of my principles, which were the common ones, and to perceive their futility."[6]

Reid's rejoinder to Hume's scepticism is directed primarily at his theory of ideas and its consequences for the rationality of our belief in the external world. He appeals to self-evident first principles which stand in no need of rational justification and which *ceteris paribus* ought to be regarded as trustworthy. Instead of Hume's appeal to the power of the imagination which constrains us to believe in the external world, causal forces, other minds etc., Reid argues that we should trust as reliable the constitution of our human nature. The principles of common sense are those fundamental beliefs by which we regulate our conscious experience and activity in the world. They are justifiable only in the sense that they cannot be called into question without absurdity and are further characterised by universal consent, their early appearance in human cognitive development and their necessity for human practice.[7] Examples of contingent first principles include 'those things do really exist which we distinctly perceive by our senses, and are what we perceive them to be' and 'we have some degree of power over our actions, and the determinations of our will'.[8] Reid's confidence in the reliability of our most natural beliefs is clearly set within the context of his theism. He assumes everywhere that a benevolent God would not deceive us in our most fundamental beliefs about the make-up of the everyday world.[9]

The most recent and plausible defence of Reid's strategy is that offered by the American philosopher, Keith Lehrer. According to Lehrer, Reid's philosophy may be characterised as a form of 'nativism'. It is part of our natural constitution as human beings that we understand the world the way we do. To ask whether our most basic understanding of the world and ourselves is true is self-defeating since such an inquiry could only take place on the basis of principles of rationality which have already been presupposed.

"The faculties of the mind play the role of modules in contemporary psychological theory. They are elementary information processing systems, that is, systems yielding the output of conception and conviction in response to sensory input. The doxastic [belief] output of the innate principles of such systems, which are analogous to the programme of an information processing system, are the beliefs of common sense ... The basic beliefs of our faculties must be assumed to be trustworthy without argumentation, because all argumentation assumes the trustworthiness of our faculties. Nativism is the mother of common-sense epistemology."[10]

In his moral theory Reid contests Hume's claim that ethical evaluations reduce to feelings of the subject rather than judgments of an object. There are according to Reid two rational principles of action with which our nature has endowed us: self-interest and duty. It is through a sense of duty that human beings are able to distinguish between right and wrong courses of action. This moral discrimination is no less genuine than other forms of intellectual judgement. "[I]t is not more evident, that there is a real distinction between true and false, in matters of speculation, than that there is a real distinction between right and wrong in human conduct."[11]

The notion of duty, according to Reid, is *sui generis*. It cannot be cashed out into some more primitive concept, e.g. self-interest or happiness. It can only be defined by synonymous words or phrases such as "what we ought to do, what is fair and honest, what is approvable, what every man professes to be the rule of his conduct, what all men praise, and what is in itself laudable, though no man should praise it".[12] If we were to pose the ancient question of Glaucon in Plato's *Republic* - why should I be moral?- Reid would appeal to every human being's sense of honour. This is a basic principle of our nature and cannot be resolved into regard for one's reputation or any other non-moral category.

> "Ask the man of honour, why he thinks himself obliged
> to pay a debt of honour? The very question shocks him.
> To suppose that he needs any other inducement to do it
> but the principle of honour, is to suppose that he has no
> honour, no worth, and deserves no esteem.
> "There is therefore a principle in man, which, when he
> acts according to it, gives him a consciousness of worth,
> and when he acts contrary to it, a sense of demerit."[13]

Moral obligation is neither a quality of an action nor of an agent. It is a fundamental relation between the two which cannot be resolved to admit of any further definition. It is a relation which depends upon the voluntary nature of action, and also the understanding and will of the agent. In the absence of these, moral responsibility cannot be assumed. We are aware of obligation through a moral sense or faculty with which nature has endowed us. The deliverances of our conscience are as ineluctable as the deliverances of the five physical senses. Reid makes no attempt to disguise the intended theistic context of this assertion. "The Supreme Being, who has given us eyes to discern what may be useful and what hurtful to our natural life, hath also given us this light within to direct our moral conduct."[14] Moreover, Reid is confident that the moral sense can inform us that God in his benevolence and wisdom will ensure the final reward of the righteous. "While the world is under a wise and benevolent administration, it is impossible that any man should, in the issue, be a loser by doing his duty."[15]

Reid's insistence upon an innate and divinely-bestowed moral sense was accompanied by an emphasis upon the significance of moral training and the presence of moral diversity across time and space. In this connection he is again able to press the analogy with other forms of judgement. As in mathematics and science much instruction is necessary for true perception, so, in matters of moral judgement, training is crucial. The presence of moral diversity and error does not disconfirm his moral sense theory. We find abundant error in other forms of perception but this does not prevent us from judging that there is a truth of the matter even though it eludes the grasp of many. Reid shows a healthy awareness of the significance of moral training and example. "Our natural power of discerning between right and wrong needs the aid of instruction, education, exercise, and habit as well as our other natural powers."[16]

The particular principles of virtue are enunciated by Reid under five headings, and we can inspect each of these in due course:[17]

1) "We ought to prefer a greater good, though more distant to a less; and less evil to a greater." Reid here draws attention to such virtues as temperance, prudence, courage and justice by which human beings habitually seek the greater good even when this entails sacrificing a lesser.

2) "As far as the intention of nature appears in the constitution of man, we ought to comply with that intention, and to act agreeably to it." This appeal to something like Stoic and natural law teaching argues that the command of God is written on human

hearts and cannot be disobeyed without human beings acting against the intention of nature. The benevolence of nature is seen in our propensity toward self-preservation, to seek knowledge, to show affection toward children, toward our near relations and the communities to which we belong.

3) "No man is born for himself only." We find ourselves bound to other people in a variety of ways and we owe social obligation not only to family and friends, but to neighbourhood, country and humanity as a whole. This axiom informs all the social virtues.

4) "What we approve in others, that we ought to practice in like circumstances, and what we condemn in others we ought not to do." Reid's version of the Golden Rule is supported by reference to the theological conviction that God's relation to each human being is morally equivalent. Of all the rules of morality this is the most comprehensive and "truly deserves the encomium given it by the highest authority, that it is the law and the prophets".

5) "To every man who believes the existence, the perfections, and the providence of God, the veneration and submission we owe to him is self-evident." Reid confidently appeals to the sanctions of religion in his list of the particular principles of morals.

The influence of Reid's common-sense realism was considerable upon Scottish, French and American thought in the nineteenth century. In Scotland, his work was taken up and adapted in the more sophisticated philosophy of Sir William Hamilton, and it found favour even in the evangelical theology of Thomas Chalmers. In France it was discovered by Royer-Collard and Victor Cousin and influenced educational policy for much of the nineteenth century. It was exported to the USA by ex-patriots - notably, John Witherspoon, the sixth President of Princeton - and it flourished as the most suitable handmaid to theology in the work of the Hodges and others. Its attractions for theology were multifarious. It provided the defender of the faith with an apologetic weapon to attack the forces of unbelief. The existence of God and the deliverances of conscience could be established independently of revelation, and thus the sceptic could be challenged without resort to special pleading. At the same time, unlike the work of Kant and Hegel, Reid's philosophy did not threaten theology. There was little danger of the truths of revelation being dominated by a constrictive conceptuality. In short, Scottish common-sense realism gave Calvinist theologians all that they needed and nothing more.[18]

But can Reid's philosophy still speak to the more pluralist and fragmented moral world of the late twentieth century? Does it provide an adequate response to the many forms of moral relativism which Michael Novak has described as "an invisible gas, odourless, deadly, that is now polluting every free society on earth, a gas that attacks the central nervous system of moral striving"?[19] When one examines Reid's particular moral principles one is immediately struck by the implausibility of the fifth as a self-evident principle. "To every man who believes the existence, the perfections, and the providence of God, the veneration and submission we owe to him is self-evident." Even those of us who today continue to affirm the existence, perfections and providence of God would be unlikely to claim this as a self-evident truth in any Reidian sense. At any rate, as a theistic affirmation it now looks very odd in the company of the four previous principles which still have a measure of *prima facie* plausibility. The pluralism of contemporary society has made us deeply conscious both of the ways in which many find their moral bearing without reference to religion, and also of the divergent concepts of God which divide those who do seek such reference. Reid's proposal and the theistic context of his epistemology look too redolent of the provincialism and optimism of the Scottish enlightenment.

This observation leads to the wider criticism of Reid's moral theory that he takes insufficient account of the contextuality of moral judgments. The values we hold reflect the traditions we inherit, the communities we belong to, and the codes of conduct that we have been brought up to observe. Reid's philosophy, by contrast, suggests that by the light of nature we all acknowledge a set of common moral principles from which we can deduce how we ought to act in particular circumstances. The most powerful statement of this criticism is made by Alasdair MacIntyre.

"Agreement in fundamental principles does not on

Reid's view derive either from agreement in passion and sentiment embodied in institutionalised exchanges or from an education in the virtues only to be provided by some one particular type of community; such agreement is not in fact derivative. All plain persons of sound mind assent to one and the same set of fundamental truths as underived first principles, the truths of common sense, as soon as these truths are elicited from the mind by experience."[20]

Yet MacIntyre's criticism of Reid arguably ignores the extent to which the necessity of moral and intellectual training dominates Reid's writings. A self-evident principle is not necessarily self-evident to all people; it is known as such only by those who have submitted themselves to the discipline of training in a particular field. The skills of perceiving moral truths are acquired by those who are socially sensitised, and without such nurture moral judgement and the power of reasoning would be absent from human life.[21] Reid observes the necessity of such nurture throughout all of nature. He is even capable of the more Augustinian remark that such is the corruption in moral perception throughout humankind that divine revelation has become necessary.[22]

In defence of Reid one might draw attention to the continuing plausibility of principles 2, 3 and 4. The Golden Rule - do to others as you would have them do to you - is a moral precept that is more widespread than the province of the Judaeo-Christian tradition. As a universal moral truth it informs all the world's major religious traditions, and places important restraints upon acceptable conduct.[23] The relational and societal nature of human life is increasingly acknowledged for its anthropological and moral significance. We depend upon others not only for our survival but for our psychological, moral and spiritual well-being. Furthermore, there is also much evidence to support the Reidian conviction that justice is a natural rather than an artificial virtue. The UN Declaration on Human Rights and the widespread (albeit often impotent) outrage at the abuse of such rights throughout the world suggest that the requirements of justice are more than variant social contrivances. We want to say that these are embedded in our constitution as moral beings and in the fabric of our world, and whatever problems surround these strange notions we are reluctant ever to abandon them.

Even in a 'pluralist' society we need to be reminded of those moral platitudes that are present in popular opinion, in the media, in political discourse and in the way our children are educated at school and university. As platitudes they often go unnoticed, yet set definite limits to the acceptable degrees of diversity. In this context Jeffrey Stout has drawn attention to the moral world of the nursery in liberal democratic societies. The social skills that our children are taught from the earliest stage create a capacity for the forming of friendships and instil a moral code which includes the importance of fair play, truthfulness, benevolence and of showing courtesy towards strangers irrespective of colour or race.[24] If this description fits our contemporary condition we must enquire as to the origin and justification of these platitudes.

Thomas Reid's insistence upon some fundamental moral judgments as innate and true remains an important attempt to articulate some of our most deeply-held intuitions. His arguments merit continued interest if only because any departure from a belief in the objectivity of ethical judgments threatens the seriousness most of us wish to attach to moral education and endeavour.

8

BETWEEN LEGALISM AND LIBERALISM: WISDOM IN CHRISTIAN ETHICS

Iain Torrance

The General Assembly of the Church of Scotland of 1994 received the report of the Panel on Doctrine's Working Party on "The Theology of Marriage". The Report of the Working Party was produced under the convenership of Mrs Elizabeth Templeton, a lay free-lance theologian living in Edinburgh. The Report, both in the proposals it made and in its potential for creating future discord, is one of the most controversial ever to be submitted to the General Assembly. This is what makes it of wider interest. Although it focusses on the issue of sexual ethics, in the background there lie the broader issues of the self-understanding of a Reformed Church, the authority and status of the Bible in such a Church, and a modern version of the perennial clash between law and grace.

The controversial nature of the Report meant that it was loved by the Press. Yet it can be argued that the Press played a necessary (and correct) role. Assembly rules made no provision for the presentation of a minority report, and the Panel had been split 8 - 6 in its decision to send the Report to the Assembly. Dissenters on the Panel were allowed only some 300 words in the Panel's Report with which to make their criticism. As a result they felt obliged to produce a pamphlet (*Why Dissent?*), and the *Glasgow Herald* carried further criticism. Discussion tended to polarise, and lines were drawn artificially - as they have been in other such debates - between stereotyped Liberals and Conservative Evangelicals.

The aim of this short study is twofold: to try to begin a process of healing at the local level; to try to address constructively the more intractable problem of *the application* of grace. The issues are enormous and of vital importance not just for the future of the Church of Scotland. Each side must acknowledge the strengths of what the other is saying. Each side must learn to be less omnivorous in its claims. Characteristically, Christian ethics has understood its role as being both to rebuke and to exhort. I suggest this undervalues the place of *forgiveness* and want to suggest the possibility of a mediating approach.

What new proposals did the Report recommend? *Deliverance 9* of the Report asked the Assembly to "Affirm love, trust, forgiveness and faithfulness as the most significant criteria by which all relationships are to be assessed; and urge congregations not to discriminate against any person on grounds of marital status or sexual orientation". This Deliverance was perceived as the crucial innovation of the Report. Every word of it is important.

How was this proposal reached? The Report points to changes both in society and in the handling of Scripture. With regard to society, it cites a number of statistics. There are changing perceptions of marriage and other sexual relationships in the late 20th century: of cohabiting couples in the UK, only 61% are married; "alternative patterns of relationship to heterosexual marriage (e.g. living together, same-sex partnerships etc) are chosen by some Christian people with no sense of guilt or shame ... "; it claims that for those born between 1966 and 1975 fewer than 1% delay their first sexual experience until marriage; it claims that a gulf has opened up between the Church's traditional teaching and the views of many younger church members. In relation to Scripture, it allows that "All of us within the Church of Scotland believe Scripture to be the supreme rule of faith and life". The divisions occur over how we hear and understand and handle that supreme rule. The Report lays stress on the insight that all human understandings are contextual: they are relative to the specific cultural context in which people operate. And we may well be locked into our cultures: even if key Biblical passages are trans-cultural, can we know that the words for extra-marital or co-marital sex *mean the same* in our society as they did in a society where women were seen partially as property? It is claimed that we now simply know more about the human personality: it is increasingly accepted that same-sex orientation is a given, not a chosen, condition.

The Report asks how we are to respond to the changing social situation. It allows that many in the Church will hold to traditional teaching and practice: marriage is between one man and one woman for life; there should be abstinence before marriage and fidelity after it. But others, it argues, will try to interpret the complexity they feel. They are aware of the danger of hypocrisy if too great a gap opens up between the Church's official statements on sexuality and the way it deals with matters at a pastoral level. It allows that there is a range of responses. Charles Davis is quoted: "Where pluralism is denied, finitude is forgotten, and faith is corrupted into an idolatrous absolutising of one of its particular expressions". In this spirit, the Report points to a "core gospel" which appears to outweigh particular texts or biblically tolerated practices (like slavery). It believes that all Christians can unite in maintaining that sexuality is not to be reduced to sport, entertainment or a means for selfish ends. Building on this, it looks for the recovery of a more widely conceived chastity as a basic virtue in Christian sexual ethics. "Chastity exists within relationships, not only as a negative value of abstinence but as a deep and inherently affirmative moral value, involving integrity, loyalty, fidelity and purity of heart together ... it is invariably violated by casual, promiscuous or exploitative sex. It is less clear that it is threatened by the mutual self-giving of two people who love each other and hope to make a life together." In this spirit the Report goes on to suggest that if free, mutual giving and receiving of selfhood is the glory of marriage between man and woman, it is harder to deny "a comparable wholeness" to people of same-sex orientation where these qualities are present. It quotes a gay Christian who affirms his belief that "a relationship which displays the quality of love as understood in an appropriate Christian way is as acceptable an expression of their God-given natures as heterosexual people enjoy in their relationships ... ".

The Panel's dissenters set themselves to produce criticism, not an alternative report, so what they said was inevitably negative rather than constructive. They argued that the Report, no matter what it alleged, had no clear understanding of the Bible *as an authority*, rather than as merely suggestive. We are led into *an unending conversation* with the Bible rather than into convictions. This led to the accusation that the Report had sold out to the Spirit of the Age. "Since when did *the quantity* of sin make that which was done right?" Mrs Templeton was asked at the Assembly. The Report, by stressing *criteria of quality* (love, trust, freedom, mutuality) to determine the worth of sexual acts, neglected *criteria of appropriateness* (the doctrine of creation). The Report's assertion that even Christians who enter into non-marital relationships may not accept the traditional evaluation of their lifestyle as morally wrong, *or a matter for repentance and change*, led to the accusation that its presupposition was a vacuous, secularised love which merely affirmed the status quo. This would be a cheap grace which neglected the challenge and summons of the Gospel. There is a long tradition (exemplified by PT Forsyth) that the love of God is a *holy* love. It was argued that here the Report betrayed the fact that it had little or no understanding of ecclesiology. It was claimed that the Report's stress upon the criteria of quality to determine the worth of a sexual act was of little pastoral use. How do you quantify such abstract criteria? When do we ever know if *enough* love, trust, freedom and mutuality are present? Adding the criterion "fidelity" does not rescue the Report, as it is not evident that fidelity of itself necessarily implies *exclusivity* (polygamous unions may be very faithful). Because of its use of unquantifiable criteria, the Report was accused of stepping on to a slippery slope. It was alleged that, in extreme cases, criteria of quality in the absence of criteria of appropriateness could not rule out incest (or explain satisfactorily why it is wrong). The Report was accused of arguing effectively for the *moral equivalence* of a variety of sexual acts (pre-marital, post-marital, homosexual and heterosexual) if the same criteria of quality were found to apply. It was claimed that such an argument had Trojan horse qualities. Once it was accepted, one no longer had a moral vocabulary with which to comment on questions like whether or not lesbian couples should be permitted to bear children by IVF. The moral equivalence argument is sometimes presented under the guise of an appeal to equal rights. But it was objected that this is another dubious argument: you cannot argue for the equal right of something until you have first proved it is morally equivalent, and that is the point at issue. Finally, it was argued that the Report is imbued with a naive 1960s optimism which predates modern disclosures (not understandings) of abuse. Camille Paglia's uncomfortable assertion comes to mind: "whenever sexual freedom is sought or achieved, sadomasochism will not be far behind ... Sex is a far darker power than feminism has admitted".

These arguments are telling, but it cannot be said that the critics have it all their own way. There are questions which they, too, must address. It is undeniable that convenient and almost-certain contraception is new and brings different moral questions. These must be faced: where it is stripped of its procreational aspect, how are we to evaluate sexual contact? There simply is not the same fear of producing a baby that there was 30 years ago. We understand now much more clearly that there is no text without a community, no ethic without a sociology. It follows that it is undeniable that there are different ways of reading the Bible in sincerity and we must acknowledge our cultural rootedness and the limitations of our particular standpoints. Although human sexual orientation is still a mystery, the bulk of the available evidence seems to indicate that it is a given (possibly genetic) condition, not chosen. The traditional teaching that marriage is between one man and one woman for life, with abstinence before and faithfulness after, does little to equip us pastorally for a situation in which certainly a third of marriages end in divorce and very many couples never marry. The Roman Catholic moral theologian Kevin Kelly once wrote that Christianity has an ethic *of marriage* but not of sex. The furore over the Panel's Report obliges us to ask if he was right: does Christianity have a vocabulary with which it can grapple with sex or can it *only* speak of marriage?

These difficulties point to an area where *neither* side is entirely sure-footed. The 'Liberals' genuinely wish to make the presence of love and grace the primary criteria for what is right: to see the good and affirm it in even the most fractured and unexpected relationships. The 'Traditionalists' accuse them of cheap grace; of selling Christianity out to the Spirit of the Age; of standing on a slippery slope (the incest argument; the adultery as part of a "greater faithfulness" argument); of turning the Bible into a nose of wax. The 'Liberals' counterclaim that unless one steps on to the slippery slope, one turns one's back on the now more complex world; one *only* speaks the language of Zion (Christianity becomes a ghetto); one turns the Gospel into an ethic of control; one multiplies and magnifies guilt.

How can one move past this impasse? It is a major challenge to *Christian* ethics. What we need is a way to express Christian discrimination (and exhortation) without thereby inevitably and necessarily demonising everything else. Has this been achieved elsewhere in Christian ethics? I suggest we see an approach towards this in our evolving attitudes to abortion and divorce. The Church as Church must always, I believe, view abortion as an evil and a tragedy. But it must also recognise that sometimes that is all, or the best that can happen. If we are not to be impossibly legalistic, we need (in faith) to step on to the slippery slope (the merit of the 'Liberals'), but we need to find clear ways of not polishing the ice (the merit of the 'Traditionalists'). Yet, if those clear ways of putting on the brakes are themselves made *over explicit* and formalised, we simply construct a new legalism, and effectively step off the slope again. The urgency of the Gospel obliges us to step on to the slope: how are we neither to polish the ice, nor lapse into legalism at a more refined level? What we need are *inspecific criteria*, and if this is not to be impossibly fuzzy, we need to find *a logic* for this kind of discourse.

It is here that we may find real help in the remarkably fertile and profound Gifford Lectures delivered by Michael Polanyi in the University of Aberdeen in 1951-2, and later published under the title *Personal Knowledge* (London, Routledge & Kegan Paul, 1958). The continuing ability of Polanyi's lectures to shed light on new issues is something to celebrate in the University's quincentenary year.

Among other things, Polanyi had in his sights the Positivism which was becoming dominant in the 1940s, and which still casts a shadow on the theology of the 90s. Here, a "law of nature" marked a generality noted by the observer, rather than a regularity actually in the external world. "Laws" mapped sameness and provided both explanation of the past and prediction of the future as individual events were brought under them. The covering law both identified an event and explained it. There could be no event which was not covered by law. Such an event would be unidentifiable and unexplainable. Polanyi's concern was that this perspective created a split between theory (law) and the empirical realm upon which theory was applied, with the result that theory (law) became over-explicit (formalised), inflexible and difficult to apply in practice.

Polanyi challenged this abstract and formalised understanding of law by engaging in a re-examination of actual scientific *practice*, especially the application of skills (in chapter 4 of *Personal Knowledge*), to subvert the prevailing understanding that science (or any knowledge) proceeds through the procrustean application of rigid laws. Essentially, he argued that in a skill (informed action), the practitioner wears her learning lightly, in the sense that it is neither explicit, nor tightly formalised, nor even the focus of attention. He illustrates this. The "touch" of a concert pianist is that musician's greatest gift. But it is extremely difficult to describe exactly (in terms of theory or "law") what "touch" is. As Polanyi argues: "... the effect of the hammer on the chord is fully determined by the speed of the hammer ... As this speed varies, the note of the chord will sound more or less loudly ... it should make no difference in what manner the hammer acquired any particular speed. Accordingly, there could be no difference as between tyro and virtuoso in the tone of the notes ... " (p 50). But there is a difference, and Polanyi argued that the performed skill is more than the sum of its parts. It is not totally formalisable; it may not be made totally explicit. Why is this? Polanyi suggested that, in informed (practical) action, we have two kinds of awareness: focal and subsidiary. At an abstract level, the pianist is aware of the physics of the activity: the speed and pressure of her fingers. Equally, she is aware of the musical theory: the sequence of notes and chords which make up a composition. But all of this is given only subsidiary awareness. She looks *through* it to the compound activity of producing music, which is what is given focal awareness. The two awarenesses go together in the application of a skill, or any informed activity. This analysis (and he gave many examples) allowed Polanyi to reformulate the relation of the theoretical (law) to that to which it applied. Rather than law being an abstract, a projection from the side of the observer, Polanyi argues that the theoretical is only applicable when it is pursued in dialogue with the empirical (the two awarenesses go together). This offers a new understanding of law. Rather than being abstract, separated and imposed, law (or theory) is *unitary* and *realist* (that is, in dialogue with that to which it is applied). As such it is open-textured, flexible and not fully specifiable. Yet, at the same time, being in dialogue with that to which it relates, for all its open-textured nature, it is *not* arbitrary, it is not without limits, and crucially, it is concerned to express *what it discovers rather than what it creates*. This is a realist, unitary (not abstract) understanding of law. Though flexible, it has criteria which arise from within the actual dialogue with the object of study. To express the application of this unitary understanding of law, Polanyi used the words "connoisseurship" and "wisdom". This offers the possibility of a new understanding of what we call "natural law".

Much needs to be worked out in detail, but I would maintain that here Polanyi offers us the bones of a workable "grammar" which is promising for Christian ethics. The 'Liberals' saw the need to step out from previous certainties on to the slippery slope. But once on the ice, operating with an abstracted understanding of love and equally abstract criteria of quality control, they find it difficult to stand still. Polanyi should point them back to realism (which is the baby they threw out with the bath water). The 'Traditionalists' are equally abstract, directing their primary focus on to an abstracted law (the cuckoo *they* put into the nest). They thus find it hard to adapt to changes in reality, and lack a mechanism either to make exceptions *or to forgive*. In their different ways, each is as legalistic as the other, because each tends to operate in abstraction from the reality they address. What Polanyi suggests is that *the grammar* of Christian ethics may be couched in terms of *wisdom*, not law.

9

MARRYING WISDOM AND WITNESS
A NEW FOUNDATION FOR
PRACTICAL THEOLOGY

William Forbes Storrar

Where do the foundations of Practical Theology lie at Aberdeen? A separate church chair at Christ's College was first held by David Cairns as recently as 1945, although the subject was recognised and taught in the earlier decades of this century, in both the College and the Church of Scotland's Pastoral Institute in Aberdeen. The wider academic discipline itself grew out of the work of ministerial formation from the later 18th century in Europe. Wolfhart Pannenberg, however, in stressing the fundamental importance of missiology for Practical Theology, offers a new perspective on the discipline and its origins, not least at Aberdeen. The renaissance Christian humanist tradition embodied by Erasmus, which shaped Bishop Elphinstone's new university in 1495, also found in that great scholar an early and eloquent advocate of mission in the lands beyond Christendom after 1492. That wedding of humanism and evangelism, considered in this essay, offers us a new foundation for Practical Theology.

With few exceptions, little has been done to consider the implications of Pannenberg's missiological axiom for the history and the future of the discipline. One notable response is the work of Duncan Forrester. In his inaugural lecture as the Professor of Christian Ethics and Practical Theology at Edinburgh University, Forrester acknowledged that his post was the successor to the nineteenth century chair of Evangelistic Theology at New College, founded in 1867. This was the first chair of missiology in the world and first held by the pioneer missionary statesman in India, Alexander Duff:

> "He was the founder of the theological study of
> missiology which, as Pannenberg has reminded us, is
> of fundamental importance to Practical Theology, and

constantly reminds us that Christian practice must be understood within the horizon of the Kingdom into which men and women of every tribe and tongue and people and nation are at the last to be gathered."[1]

Aberdeen can lay claim to a modest but legitimate share in this missiological tradition. Duff's professorship was a peripatetic one that involved him in teaching his mission course in the three Free Church of Scotland Colleges; including the one in Aberdeen which later became known as Christ's College and which united with the University Divinity Faculty after 1929. Duff taught in Aberdeen in a four week intensive course in March of each year from 1867 to 1878. And yet Aberdeen's links with missiology lie much earlier than the nineteenth century, in the new learning and the new horizons of King's College after 1495. As the work of historians like Leslie Macfarlane and John Durkan has documented, Bishop Elphinstone founded a humanist university that gave the North of Scotland a window on the wider world.[2]

The View from King's: Europe is a Very Small Part of the World

Pannenberg has argued that the mission directed to all mankind is not simply the practice which originally created the church, but also the ultimate horizon on which the whole life of the church must be understood.[3] This last statement would have come as little surprise to the first Arts students at King's College. They pursued their third year studies in geography amid the excitement and stimulus of Christopher Columbus' voyage to what he assumed to be the Indies in 1492. The second Principal of King's, William Hay, possessed a copy of Amerigo Vespucci's account of his own voyages to what he argued was in fact a 'New World', the Americas. It is likely that Hay used this text, *Quattuor Americi Navigationes*, the four voyages of Amerigo Vespucci, to instruct his students on this new physical and mental horizon for Christendom. Hay at least would be aware that the 'discovery' of the New World was creating a lively intellectual debate across Europe.

Theologians and legal theorists wrestled with the status of

the indigenous peoples and cultures of the Americas under the
Spanish conquest and Catholic mission. The New World was
demanding not only a new cartography but a new moral geography of the identity and boundaries of humanity. It may be argued that Practical Theology, in missiological embryo, was conceived out of the union of humanism and evangelism which
occured during that early sixteenth century debate. The match-
maker was Erasmus.

As Patrick Edwards has noted in an earlier essay in this volume, Erasmus was read and appreciated in Old Aberdeen. Both
Hay and Hector Boece, first Principal of King's, were Christian
humanist scholars in their own right, combining devout Christian piety with the new learning of humanist studies. They held
Erasmus in the highest regard. Indeed, Boece was a fellow student in Paris and remained a friend and correspondent, Erasmus
dedicating a poem to him, *The Room Where Jesus was Born*, in
his very first book, published in 1496. In 1535 Erasmus published one of his last works, *Ecclesiastes sive De Ratione
Concionandi*, a study 'On Preaching' in four books. The introduction to the modern Latin edition of this text suggests that
there could be no more appropriate subject for a profound syn-
thesis of the two central themes around which Erasmus' work
revolves, humanist learning and the philosophy of Christ, than
this treatise on the eloquence of the pulpit.

In James Weiss' judgement, this handbook of Christian rhetoric became Erasmus' means to recapitulate his life's work. For
our purposes the significance of this long neglected work lies in
his emphasis on the expanding global horizon of Christian mission as the context for preaching. Leon-Ernest Halkin has observed that, "The mental world of the humanists was not that of
Aristotle and Cicero ... it was the contemporary world of ...
Christopher Columbus".[4] And Erasmus himself writes, with
Christendom's discovery of the 'New World' of the Americas
in mind:

"Europe is a very small part of the world .... It cannot be
doubted that in such an immense territory there are rough
and simple peoples who could easily be won over to
Christ if men were sent to sow good seed. What of the

fact that every day lands hitherto unknown are being discovered and, it is rumoured, there are more beside which none of our people have yet reached?"[5]

This was the perception of the world that the first humanist teachers offered their students at Aberdeen. It was a perception that Erasmus turned into what Olav Myklebust has called 'a passionate appeal to the clergy of the Church to engage in the work of foreign mission'.[6] Erasmus, the friend of mission and the friend of Hector Boece, offered in his book on preaching a new Christian humanist foundation for evangelism. He placed his reflections on 'evangelical oratory' and ministerial training in the context of scholarly reflection on mission and its practice in the world beyond Christendom. In doing so, Erasmus anticipated the kind of Practical Theology called for by Pannenberg and taught in Aberdeen today. That would have pleased his friend Hector Boece.

In a letter to Erasmus, Boece once remarked, "I myself will make it my endeavour to the utmost of my ability, to see that those who are being trained in Aberdeen in character and learning shall revere your name." In as much as the study of missiology is central to the Practical Theology curriculum at Aberdeen University in 1995, as Erasmus called for in his handbook on preaching in 1535, it may be said that we continue to honour a pledge made almost five hundred years ago. More than that, we continue to pursue Erasmian concerns in an Aberdeen tradition which in the twentieth century has produced its own neglected theologian of global mission, David S Cairns (1862-1946).

In Erasmus and Cairns, in the first and most recent centuries of Aberdeen's five hundred year tradition, we find Christian thinkers who offer us a new narrative for Practical Theology. It becomes the story of the Church's wrestling with the practice of Christian mission on the margins of a changing world. As Cairns argued, it deals with a faith and a mission that rebel against sin, suffering and evil.[7] In this sense, Practical Theology seeks to sustain the logic of the disorientating practice of Jesus. His ministry embraced into God's Kingdom those whom the ancient world saw as the marginal non-persons of Israel and Rome and so committed his disciples to a revolutionary moral geography.

Practical Theology's distinctive missiological task is to bring the unseen edges of the world into the centre of theological reflection on Christian practice. Its role within church, university and society today is a de-stabilising one: to overturn secure maps of reality that so often leave out forgotten majority members of humanity, like women and the poor and neglected parts of the earth, like the Two Thirds World. The precedent for this lies with Erasmus.

A True, Effective and Genuine Theology of Practice

Erasmus, the most prominent Christian humanist in renaissance Europe, had long been a public voice for peaceful evangelisation rather than the violent conquest of the Turks and peoples beyond the boundaries of Christendom. He wrote, in the 1518 preface to *The Handbook of the Christian Soldier*, that the best way to defeat the Turks was to make them realise that Christians were not greedy for their empire or wealth but sought only their salvation and the glory of Christ.

For Erasmus, such a just and peaceful witness to Christ 'is the true and effective and genuine theology, which long ago made proud philosophers and unconquered monarchs bow the knee to Christ. If this and this alone could be our purpose, Christ himself will be at our side'. It was in his book on preaching, *Ecclesiastes*, that Erasmus developed this idea of the truth of theology as something rooted in the persuasive, non-coercive practice of Christian mission. He worked on this book for many years after its inception in 1519, and only published it in the year before his own death, in 1536. This is a work of lasting significance, a *locus classicus* in the missiological history and identity of Practical Theology.

In four books Erasmus brings all the skills of classical humanist rhetoric and his biblical studies to the greater service of preaching, a vocation for which he has the highest regard. In that *Ecclesiastes* is a study of preaching, it rightly falls within the traditional history of Practical Theology; as the study of the vocational duties of priests and ministers in the church, including homiletics along with liturgics, catechetics and pastoralia. Yet Erasmus himself subverts this safe ecclesial and clerical context for preaching and Christian practice. The truest work of preaching is done when the preacher sows the seed among those who have never heard the Gospel, in the new world beyond the borders of Christendom, evangelising rather than exploiting its peoples:

> "There is no lack of proclaimers of God's word in the cities. But the noblest calling is to sow the seed where no one else is sowing - in desolate districts, in barbarous regions where the seedground is vast but there is none to till the soil."[8]

This requires an appropriate education for missionary preachers. As Weiss comments, in his wide-ranging study of preaching Erasmus "held forth on the training of the clergy, relating it at one point to the proper ends of voyages of discovery".[9] I wish to argue for the theological significance of this comparison. Erasmus' work on preaching anticipates, at this key point, Pannenberg's axiom that missiology is of fundamental importance for the theology of practice, not least the practice of ministry.

There are four Christian humanist themes that are fundamental to Erasmus' rhetorical arguments in support of mission, in the section of Book One of *Ecclesiastes* where he links preaching to evangelism. Mission is inseparable from peace and justice, the integrity of Christian practice, the renewal of the church and the role of education.[10] All four themes serve to shape the kind of missionary encounter with the new world which he advocated. The first theme lies at the heart of Erasmus' Christian humanist concern for mission, while the other three themes are best considered together as dimensions of his one theological concern to consider all Christian and human practice from the perspective of mission.

A Peaceful Evangelism

First, for Erasmus mission is inseparable from the Gospel call to peace and justice. He condemns those Christian princes who impose the yoke of oppression rather than the sweet yoke of Christ on their non-Christian subjects (328-33); and who prevent missionaries from evangelising such people, "fearing lest if their subjects gain a little wisdom they may cast off the heavy yoke that oppresses them" (345-9). Above all, it is the duty of the Christian prince to support the task of mission through striving for peace, suppressing lawlessness and providing "incorruptible magistrates and judges" (554-6). He uses the contrast between the violent and greedy exploitation of the New World and its peaceful evangelisation to argue for authentic Christian practice (356-62).

The Christian encounter with new lands and peoples should be characterised by peaceful and just practice. This Erasmian plea stands in stark contrast with the actual practice of the Spanish conquistadors and colonists in the Americas. And yet it was a plea that did not go unheard in the New World. The Puerto Rican historian Luis Rivera has described Spain's political and religious conquest of the Americas as "a violent evangelism". Theological justification was given for denying the equal humanity of its indigenous peoples, seizing their lands and forcing their conversion. There were, however, Spanish Christians who opposed this brutal conquest of the Indians and defended their humanity and rights in the name of the Gospel. The most influential among them was Bartolomé de Las Casas, bishop of Chiapas, Guatemala, and a passionate advocate of the liberation of the native peoples from Spanish oppression.

Rivera notes the probable influence of Erasmus on Las Casas' commitment to peaceful and just evangelism in the Americas.[11] It should also be noted that several of the Catholic missionary orders, not least the Jesuits, did practise such a peaceful evangelism in identifying with the peoples and cultures of South America and Asia. Erasmus' characteristic Christian humanist concern for peacemaking, so notable a feature of the lives of Bishop William Elphinstone and Hector Boece, helped to shape a view of mission that was inseparable from the practice of justice and peaceful evangelism on the shifting frontiers of Christendom.

A Critical Missiology

In his book on preaching, not only does Erasmus make this case for peaceful evangelism. He also uses his missiological perspective to develop his own theology of practice, combining his three other distinctive Christian humanist concerns for godliness, renewal and learning. He offers a critical missiology that raises fundamental questions for all areas of practical theology, especially spirituality, church reform and education for ministry.

Along with a passion for peace, Erasmus has a second concern for the integrity of Christian practice. Echoing the humanist cry *ad fontes* he draws on the pure sources of the Gospels and the New Testament, especially the story of the labourers and the harvest in Matthew 9:35-38, and the missionary life of Paul in the Epistles. Preaching the Gospel in lands that have never heard it will require godly preachers like Paul whose life and message are one. Such missionary preaching will demand sacrificial Christian living, even death. Evangelists must offer those to whom they preach a whole Gospel to meet all their needs, "For it is in the end the mark of a true shepherd to offer threefold nourishment - holy doctrine, holy life and bodily sustenance" (533-4).

Thirdly, the biblical call to mission is used by Erasmus to expose the failures in the practice and piety of the contemporary Church and the need for church reform (453-517). The Church must address the spiritual and structural problems in its own life that have left it ill-prepared to meet the missionary challenge of the New World. Mission requires the renewal of the laity and the reform of the religious orders.

Finally, Erasmus sees education as the key to mission and the renewal of the preaching ministry in the Church. At a practical level, mission requires learning foreign languages in order to "teach the Word of God among barbarian races" (370-1). Erasmus the pedagogue believes that every educational barrier may be overcome. If elephants can be taught to dance for the amusement of monarchs, then surely the ruler of the Church can attract and train preachers to serve Christ (338-41)! Above all, the unevangelised need to be taught the philosophy of Christ through missionary preachers (344-6). But how are such missionary educators to be trained for this vital task? For Erasmus this is the responsibility of the bishop:

"Bishops will provide us with clerics of orderly life, they will give us preachers endued with the evangelical virtues; to mould our youth they will give us men who are holy and learned besides, men who will sow in tender minds the seeds of Christian holiness. Upon such persons especially is laid responsibility for the vigorous rejuvenation of the spirit of the Gospel among the people." (556-9)

There could hardly be a more fitting description of the vision of Bishop Elphinstone in founding his university to serve the cause of the Gospel and the people of the North of Scotland. As Leslie J Macfarlane has noted, his "greatest desire was that all who came to his university would be imbued with the spirit of Christian humanism and the search for wisdom which, to him, was the proper purpose of education and which alone gave meaning to it."[12] In Practical Theology at Aberdeen University today we continue to seek that Erasmian marriage of wisdom and witness which is our rich inheritance over five hundred years.

10

ABERDEEN UNIVERSITY AND THE STUDY OF RELIGIONS

James Thrower

For the greater part of its 500 year history the University of Aberdeen, like other ancient European Universities, was concerned with the study of only one religion, the Christian. Religions other than the Christian, where they were studied at all, were studied either within the context of classical studies (the religions of Greece and Rome) or within the syllabus of dogmatic and apologetic theology where, as had been the case in the Christian Church from its inception, they could conveniently be dismissed as the work of the devil.[1]

By the beginning of the nineteenth century this situation was beginning to change. The Renaissance discovery of Classical Antiquity as exhibiting an alternative way of life to the Christian, which gave European intellectuals their first experience for many centuries of a clash of world views, the exploration of the New World, increased commercial contact with the lands beyond Europe, particularly with Asia and Africa, the growth of empire, and the experience of the Christian missionary movement, taken together with the determination of many of the leading thinkers of the seventeenth and eighteenth centuries to explore 'natural' as well as 'revealed' religion, all contributed to the creation of an unprecedented interest in Europe in religions world-wide. A further development in the nineteenth century was the translation into the languages of Europe of many of the texts of Indian and Chinese religious cultures. The foundations for what, in 1867, one of the founding fathers of the academic study of religions, Freidrich Max Müller, called 'the science of religion' were beginning to be laid.

The contribution of the University of Aberdeen (rather more, it must be admitted, through a number of distinguished alumni than directly through its teachers) to the laying of those foundations was out of all proportion to both the university's size and its geographical location. It was not, however, until 1970 that the University formally admitted the study of religions into the syllabus of its MA degree.

The outstanding contribution of the Scottish Universities to the eighteenth century European *Aufklärung* is well documented and, today, universally recognised[2], and it was, as Professor Kitty Datta of the University of Jadavpur has shown, the ideals and attitudes of the Scottish Enlightenment, as exemplified in the teaching of such as James Dunbar, Professor of Moral Philosophy at Aberdeen and author of *Essays on the History of Mankind in Rude and Cultivated Ages* (1780), which inspired the activities of one of the great Scottish administrators of British India, Sir James Mackintosh, who graduated from Aberdeen in 1784. Shortly after arriving in Bombay in 1804, Mackintosh founded the Literary (later the Asiatic) Society of Bombay, a society which had as its treasurer Mackintosh's fellow Aberdonian, the merchant Charles Forbes. Other Aberdeen alumni in the society included Theodore Forbes and the mathematician Charles Skene. Although the society's interests were less orientalist than those of its sister society in Calcutta (The Bengal Asiatic Society founded in 1784), under Mackintosh's Presidency the Bombay Society exhibited a breadth of interest that reflected the kind of education that Mackintosh had received at the Universities of Aberdeen and Edinburgh, being a blend of the scientific, the cultural-anthropological and the literary.[3] Within the field of religious studies the society supported work such as Drummond's studies of the caste system and Sir John Malcolm's studies of Sunni Islam. A further interest of the Literary Society of Bombay under Mackintosh's Presidency was the study of the cave-temples of Elephanta and Ellora. Mackintosh himself was a frequent visitor to these temples and much interested in the analysis of the various strata, Hindu, Buddhist and Jain, thus laying the foundations for the more exact studies of recent years.

Another associate of Mackintosh, who was also a graduate of Aberdeen, was Francis Irvine of Drum in Aberdeenshire. Among the topics which engaged Irvine's interest were the impact of Hinduism on Islam in India, a survey of local differences within Hinduism, Hindu borrowings from other cultures, the spread of Hinduism in south-east Asia, and what he called 'mysticism and mystical composition' in which he compared Pythagoras and the Eclectics with the Islamic Sufis. Irvine ended his career as the first (and only) European secretary of the newly established Hindu College of Calcutta, a college that was to play an important role in the 'Bengal Renaissance' of both Hindu literature and Hindu religion.

Mackintosh and Irvine have been dealt with at some length because they provide good examples of the kind of indirect influences on the growth of the academic study of religion which so often go unrecorded in official histories of the discipline. However, later in the nineteenth century, and on into the first quarter of the present century, a number of rather more well known alumni of Aberdeen University, such as James Legge (1815-1897), JF McLennan (1827-1881), William Robertson Smith (1846-1894), James Hastings (1852-1922) and John Nicol Farquhar (1861-1929)[4], were to make a more direct contribution to the academic study of religions.

James Legge was born in Huntly in Aberdeenshire in 1815 and graduated from Aberdeen with the degree of MA in 1835. After a period of theological study in London he went as a teacher to the London Missionary Society's Chinese Mission station at Malacca, where, in 1840, he was appointed Principal of the Anglo-Chinese College and where, in 1843, he negotiated the transfer of that College to the newly acquired colony of Hong Kong. He remained as Principal of the college until 1873 when he retired to England to become the first Professor of Chinese at the University of Oxford. His outstanding contribution to the study of religions was to make available to the English speaking world the religious classics of China (and not just in translation, but in scholarly editions which contained, in addition to translation, the Chinese text together with extensive notes), editions which have not, even today, outlived their utility. Publication began in 1861 with editions of *The Analects* of Confucius and of the works of Mencius and continued until his death in 1897, the final volumes being published as contributions to Max Müller's famous *Sacred Books of the East* series, to which Legge contributed six volumes in all, four covering *The Texts of Confucianism* and two *The Texts of Taoism*. Legge was a prolific writer, in both English and Chinese, and, apart from his editions of the Chinese Religious Classics, he wrote on the life and teachings of both Confucius and Mencius and also produced a comparative study of Confucianism, Taoism and Christianity. That he did not forget his former university is shown by the fact that he presented signed copies of his books as they appeared to the Aberdeen University Library. The University, in its turn, recognised the importance of his work by making him, in 1870, an honorary Doctor of Laws.

JF McLennan was born in Inverness in 1827 and graduated from Aberdeen in 1849. After further graduating from Cambridge in Mathematics and from Edinburgh in Law, he spent most of his working life not in the university world as he would have wished, but as a work-a-day lawyer in Edinburgh, although he did manage a move to London in 1870 where he became parliamentary draughtsman for Scotland, a position from which he resigned in 1875 to travel abroad. He died in 1881. He is best remembered today for putting into circulation, in a series of articles in the *Fortnightly Review* (1869-70), the term 'totemism' and for elevating this phenomenon into a full blown theory of the origin of religion, thus starting a hare which, as Eric Sharpe has noted, was not finally caught until Lévi-Strauss published his book *Le Totémisme aujourd'hui* in 1962.[5]

It was William Robertson Smith's friendship with JF McLennan, formed during Smith's time in Edinburgh, whence he had gone to study Divinity after graduating in Arts from Aberdeen in 1866, that marked the beginning of Smith's life-long interest in kinship and totemism, the results of which, when he sought to apply them to the understanding of the religion of ancient Israel, were to compound the problems that Smith, a professor at the Free Church College in Aberdeen, was having with his church. Although it was primarily his use of the methods of the German Higher Criticism that brought Smith into conflict with his Church, the issue which resulted in Smith being dismissed from his post was concerned with what Smith had said about the religion of the Hebrews in his article on 'Animal Worship' published in the *Journal of Philology* in 1880. Smith, as is well known, went on to higher things, to the editorship of the famous 9th edition of the *Encyclopaedia Britannica*, to the Lord Almoner's Readership in Arabic, the University Librarianship and, ultimately, to the Sir Thomas Adams' Professorship of Arabic at Cambridge University. It was whilst at Cambridge that Robertson Smith taught the young Reynold Nicholson (1868-1945), a graduate of Aberdeen University who himself went on to become the Sir Thomas Adams' Professor of Arabic at Cambridge, and who was one of the greatest Western students of Islam of all time.[6]

Smith's contribution to the study of religion was essentially one of method, for he was one of the first scholars to look at religion not primarily as a set of beliefs, but as a social system. In a very real sense, and no less figures than Émile Durkheim, Marcel Mauss and Sigmund Freud have acknowledged this, Smith can be regarded as the first student of religion (with the possible exception of Karl Marx) to approach religion sociologically, although Smith himself always claimed that he took this approach from McLennan. In his book *Kinship and Marriage in Early Arabia*, he wrote:

"The advantage of JF McLennan's totem hypothesis over all previous theories of primitive heathenism is that it does justice to the intimate relation between religion and the fundamental structure of society which is so characteristic of the ancient world, and that the truth of the hypothesis can be tested by observation of the social organisation as well as the religious beliefs and practices of early races."[7]

The University of Aberdeen which, it must be emphasised, had stayed on the side-lines of the Robertson Smith 'case', invited Smith, towards the end of his life, to return to Aberdeen to give its Burnett lectures. The theme that he chose was *The Religion of the Semites* and he delivered the first series of lectures between October 1888 and March 1889, the second in March 1890 and the third and last in December 1891. Unfortunately, Robertson Smith was by this time a very sick man and he died in 1894 before he could revise other than the first series for publication.[8] His influence on students of both religion and of social anthropology has been immense and even today current discussions of such topics as kinship and sacrifice invariably begin with reference to his epoch-making work.[9]

That monument to the state of knowledge about religions in the late nineteenth and early twentieth centuries, the famous, and still indispensable, twelve volume *Encyclopaedia of Religion and Ethics* (1908-1921) the aim of which in its editor's words was "to give an account of religion and ethics in all ages and in all countries of the world", was produced not in a university, but in the study of the Free Church of Scotland manse in the village of St Cyrus, some twenty miles south of Aberdeen. Its editor, James Hastings, graduated from Aberdeen in 1876. In 1884 he was ordained into the ministry of the Free Church of Scotland and his life, henceforth, was spent in the pastoral ministry of that church. Before embarking on the *Encyclopaedia* he had already produced a four volume *Dictionary of the Bible* (1898-1904), and a two volume *Dictionary of Christ and the Gospels* (1906-8) and, simultaneously with the *Encyclopaedia*, work on which was begun in 1908, he further produced a two volume *Dictionary of the Apostolic Church* (1915-18). The University of Aberdeen awarded him the honorary degree of Doctor of Divinity in 1897.

The career and achievement of the last alumnus of Aberdeen University to be considered, John Nicol Farquhar, is in every way truly remarkable. He was born in Aberdeen in 1861 and, upon leaving school, worked for a number of years as an apprentice draper in the city. At the time of his death, in 1929, he was Professor of the Comparative Study of Religions at Manchester University, and Wilde Lecturer in Natural and Comparative Religion at Oxford. His obituary notice in *The Times* stated no more than the simple truth when it claimed that "he [had done] more than any other contemporary writer to interpret to English readers the religious culture of India."[10] In the years following his apprenticeship in the Aberdeen draper's store he had returned to school at the age of twenty-one, qualified for entry into Aberdeen University (which he entered in 1882), won an open exhibition to that most aristocratic of Oxford Colleges,

Christ Church, taken a double first in 'Mods' and 'Greats', and went on to spend the greater part of his life in India, initially as a teacher with the London Missionary Society and later as Literary Secretary of the Indian YMCA. He returned to England in 1923 to become the second holder of the Chair in Comparative Religion at Manchester University. Although he was essentially a missionary theologian, - his book *The Crown of Hinduism* (1913) revolutionised missionary thinking about non-Christian religions - he did much to make contemporary Hinduism more widely known than hitherto in the West. His first book in the Comparative Study of Religions, *Gita and Gospel*, appeared in 1903, his *Primer of Hinduism* was published in 1913 and the published version of lectures which he gave in 1913 at Hartford Theological Seminary in Connecticut, USA, appeared in 1915 as *Modern Religious Movements in India*. His most enduring work, his *Outline of the Religious Literature of India*, was published in 1920. Recognition from Aberdeen came towards the end of his life with the award of an honorary Doctorate in Divinity.[11]

Although formal teaching in the study of religions had begun in many European Universities in the last quarter of the nineteenth century, it was not until 1970 that the University of Aberdeen established (in the Faculty of Arts and Social Sciences) a department of Religious Studies, although William Riddoch, a local schoolmaster[12] who died in 1942, had left the bulk of his estate to the university to establish a lectureship (and eventually he hoped a Chair) in Comparative Religion. Athough this bequest was accepted by the University Court at its meeting on 12 May 1941, it was decided to wait until the end of the War before taking the matter further and, in 1944, when the War looked like drawing to a close, it was decided to appoint a local minister, Dr WS Urquhart, who had served at one of the Scots Colleges in India, to deliver five lectures under the Riddoch bequest, for which he was to be paid fifty guineas. Dr Urquhart duly gave his lectures in the Spring of 1945 in the small chemistry classroom at Marischal college, attracting an audience of forty-two to the first lecture. He gave a second series of Riddoch lectures in 1947 after which no further Riddoch lecturers were appointed as the Court, mindful of Riddoch's wish that his bequest be used to establish a permanent lectureship, decided to add the revenue to the capital "with a view to the provision at the earliest possible date of a full-time member of staff in terms of the Testator's wishes."[13] Riddoch's Lectureship was, however, only established in 1970 with the creation of the Department of Religious Studies, the first holder being the head of the new department, Andrew Walls.

That Aberdeen was not, however, unwelcoming to the new discipline, to which, as we have seen, its own graduates had contributed so much, is illustrated by the fact that the first lecturer to be appointed to deliver Gifford Lectures in Aberdeen was none other than EB Tylor, one of the founding fathers of the academic study of religions. Tylor gave his lectures in 1889-1891. He was followed in 1891-1893 by AM Fairbairn, the Principal of the recently founded Congregational Church College in Oxford, Mansfield, and another early advocate of the Comparative Study of Religions. Twenty years earlier Fairbairn had been minister of the Evangelical Union Church in St.Paul's Street in Aberdeen, where John Nicol Farquhar had been a youthful member of his congregation.

The 'mission statement' (as it would be called today) of the newly established Department of Religious Studies in Aberdeen stated that its task was "to study religion on its own terms, and in its historical, social and phenomenological aspects." This meant that, whilst utilising such insights into religion as might be derived from history, sociology and, indeed, from any other university discipline concerned with religion, the focus of the Aberdeen department would be firmly on *religion*, even where, as in the case of Andrew Wall's colleague, the present author, the focus of study was the history of the *rejection* of religion. The 'mission statement' was also understood to mean that the remit of the department was the study of *all* the manifestations of religion and not just those found in non-Christian religions. The department, as Andrew Walls was concerned to emphasise, was most certainly *not* a department of non-Christianity.

The distinct emphases of the Aberdeen department, many of them unique both in Britain and, indeed, elsewhere in the world at that time, soon became evident. Before coming to Aberdeen Andrew Walls had worked in Africa, where he had been Head of the Department of Religious Studies at the University of Nigeria (Nsukka), and had early realised that the centre of gravity of the Christian religion was moving from Europe to Africa and Asia. It was, therefore, not surprising that one of the main areas of study in the Aberdeen department should be the study of Christianity in the Non-Western World. Walls' work in this field was augmented in the years which followed by the appointment to the department in 1972 of Harold Turner (one of the world's leading authorities on New Religious Movements in Primal Societies), and, in 1976, of the leading historian of Christianity in Africa, Adrian Hastings. The interaction of the 'primal' forms of religion (Turner always claimed that it was he who had first put the term into circulation) with the missionary religions of Christianity and Islam in Africa, Asia and, indeed, world-wide, thus became one of the major areas of study at Aberdeen. The rightness of this was shown by the number of students from Africa and Asia who came to pursue post-graduate work in the department and by the number of distinguished visitors, often on sabbatical from their home base, which the department attracted to Aberdeen.[14]

Alongside these research interests the department sought to introduce undergraduates to the whole spectrum of the world's religions (including Christian religion). An area of undergraduate study which fed into the research that was being undertaken on the interaction of primal forms of religion and the historic religions, was the study of the interaction of the religions of Northern Europe ('dead primals') with the then missionary religion of Christianity. Other areas of interest included the study of Marxist-Leninist approaches to the study of religion and, unique to Aberdeen, a course on the history of atheism. Later (from 1984-1994), the innovative nature of the study of religions in Aberdeen would again be demonstrated when David Burgess introduced one of the first courses to be taught in British universities on 'Iconography in World Religions', a course which attracted students in Arts desperate for the experience of cross-cultural study: other courses in the Study of Religions have served (and continue to serve) a similar function in a Faculty where cross-cultural studies are, even today, thinly represented.

In the mid 1980s nemesis struck. At a time when the universities of Britain were subjected to the most savage assault in their history (and this by their own government), small departments were particularly vulnerable to the pragmatism of the hour. A series of circumstances affecting the department, which the then Principal of Aberdeen University, George McNicol, called "sad, but fortuitous" (a retirement, an illness, and two migrations to fill chairs at other universities, circumstances which left only one member of the department in an established post), seemed to presage the end for the study of religions in Aberdeen, and a decision to close the Department of Religious Studies was, in fact, taken by the Senatus in 1984. One tragic consequence of the decision to close the Aberdeen department was the dismemberment (and loss to Aberdeen) of almost all of those distinct areas of study for which that department had by then acquired a world-wide reputation. Andrew Walls moved his Centre for the Study of Christianity in the Non-Western World (and its priceless archives) to Edinburgh University, where it continued to flourish to an extent where that university, having earlier established a lectureship, could move, in 1994, to create a chair in the subject. Harold Turner, failing to secure re-engagement in Aberdeen after his retirement in 1983, took his own Centre for the Study of New Religious Movements in Primal Societies (and its archives) to the Selly Oak Colleges in Birmingham. In 1993, following in the line of the distinguished alumni we have mentioned, although not himself a graduate alumnus of Aberdeen, the University did, in fact, recognise Andrew Walls' achievement by awarding him the degree of Doctor of Divinity *honoris causa*.

Yet the study of Religions survived in Aberdeen. That it did so was due in no small measure to the support that the study of religions received from the then Faculty of Divinity, which readily and willingly supported the maintenance of the teaching of Religious Studies in Arts. The Board of Studies in Divinity also opened its own syllabus more widely than had been the case hitherto to the study of religions at all levels and, in that it made certain courses in History of Religions compulsory for all Divinity students, perhaps inadvertently fulfilled one of William Riddoch's hopes when he founded his lectureship in Comparative Religion, that the courses taught from the lectureship would be compulsory for all students of Christian Divinity. Other factors contributing to the survival of the study of religions in Aberdeen were the determination of both the acting head of the department, James Thrower, and of the temporary lecturer, Dr Rosalind Shaw, that it should do so, the number of postgraduate applications from overseas that continued to pour in to the department, and the fact that the department had, before its closure, successfully bid for University Grant Commission money to mount an In-Service Training programme for teachers of Religious Studies in Scottish schools.

It was in these circumstances that generous offers from certain Arts departments in Aberdeen to take the study of religions into their own departments were (politely, but gratefully) refused. The feeling of the sole remaining established lecturer was that only within the context of Divinity could the integrity of the study of religion *as religion* be maintained and, with the support of the Faculty of Divinity and the agreement of the University, a Centre for the Study of Religions was established in 1987. In the still straitened circumstances of the 1990s it seemed a natural and logical step to integrate the Centre for the Study of Religions with an increasingly integrated Divinity Department and this took place in 1993-4. One outcome has been that the new department of Divinity with Religious Studies was invited by the Faculty of Arts and Divinity to re-establish honours teaching in Religious Studies in Arts. In 1994 the new department was given a further lectureship to strengthen teaching in the History of Religions and Malise Ruthven, a leading authority on contemporary Islam, was appointed.[15] The study of Islam, particularly in parts of the Muslim world not often studied (Africa and China), had, in fact, been a feature of the department of Religious Studies, and such noted scholars as Lamin Sanneh and Andrew Forbes, the author of the classic study, *Warlords and Muslims in Chinese Central Asia* (1986), had worked in the department.

In his book *Towards a World Theology*, the Canadian Christian theologian and student of Islam, Wilfred Cantwell Smith, roundly asserted that in the Global Village in which we now live, normative religious thought must be informed by the faiths of all humankind.[16] It is for this, if for no other reason, that theology, be it Jewish, Christian, Muslim, Hindu, Sikh or some other theology, needs the study of religions. But if theology needs the study of religions, the study of religions needs theology, for it is only within the context of the serious study of religion *qua religion*, that the study of religions can maintain its integrity and not be subsumed into the discourse of other disciplines, however relevant to the study of religion those disciplines might be. However, in that its remit is the phenomenological study of *all* religions, the Centre for the Study of Religions must continue to claim a certain amount of autonomy within a department which still (in 1994) acts both as an academic department and as a theological college of the established Church.

11

THEOLOGY AND THE IDEA OF UNIVERSITY

Jan Milič Lochman

The presence of the theological faculties within the university is not a matter of course. It is not so from the point of view of the university: there are cultural areas in which theology had been excluded from the university as in many countries in the communist era of Eastern Europe. It is not a matter of course from the perspective of theology either: there were periods of history when theology left the university in order to avoid the pressures of the totalitarian state ideology as in the days of the "*Kirchenkampf*" in Nazi Germany. For the "home" of theology is not necessarily a state institution but rather the "house" of the church. Expressed with an image taken from the theory of sculpture: "*Standbein*" (the supporting leg) of theology stands in the church, in the house of sciences its "*Spielbein*" (playing leg). However, this "play", the play of dialogical search for truth in free exchange with other intellectual disciplines, is a deeply obliging and meaningful possibility.

This possibility was envisaged in the idea of the traditional European university. The presence within the university opens for a theologian the privilege and the obligation to reflect on and critically recall the classic idea of the university.

I shall not deal with the theme in a general and abstract way. I shall pay respect to my concrete academic roots in commemorating and contemporising the spiritual vision addressing me from the foundations of my own University. The voice of the old *alma mater Basiliensis* might have something to share with its only slightly younger sister *alma mater Aberdonensis*.

Chiselled in stone on the main entrance to the University of Basle are some Latin words which greet members of the university as they enter its buildings each day: *Mortalis homo ex dono Dei per assiduum studium adispisci valet scientiae margaritam quae eum ad mundi arcana cognoscenda dilucide introducit et in infimo loco natos evehit in sublimes.*

This is an abbreviated version of the preamble to the papal bull of Pope Pius II of 12 November 1459 founding the University of Basle. In this preamble, the founder sets before his university the lofty aim of "obtaining by God's gift and assiduous study the pearl of knowledge". This knowledge "leads to a good and happy life". "It makes him who acquires it similar to God, leading him to a clear understanding of the world's mysteries ... It uplifts to the very heights those born in humblest estate."

Do these words, so plainly medieval in provenance and spirit, still have any message for our universities today? One can have respectable grounds for doubting this. The modern way - especially the modern scientific way - was largely created in conscious opposition to the spirituality and the world picture which lies behind the *magna carta of* our university. The terms of this foundation cannot be applied *in globo,* just as they stand, to our contemporary situation, still less to our plans for the future. In certain fundamental respects, however, they strike me as, *mutatis mutandis,* still extremely relevant for us today despite the abyss of time separating us from them historically. Our reflections on the theological responsibility for the idea of university may be stimulated by recalling the original motivation as reflected in this preamble. As I see it, there are three emphases which deserve our attention here.

The commendation of scientific learning

The confidence with which the preamble to the Basle foundation charter commends scientific knowledge is impressive. It assumes that knowing is basic to human nature: for human beings, the search for truth is a gift, a duty, a necessity. This is our need *and* our privilege: our need, since we cannot survive in the world at all unless we make an effort to understand it. Unlike our fellow-creatures, we are by nature extremely ill-equipped to survive. Our possibilities of life have first to be secured, and, for this, knowledge is indispensable. This is our problem. At the same time, however, it is also our privilege. In the search for knowledge and in our acquisition of knowledge, we tower above other creatures; we are closer to the angels than to the animals, equipped as we are to become autonomous and responsible agents of life.

The conviction that enquiry and knowledge are supremely important anthropologically is deeply rooted in the heart and mind of Western humanity, and this, moreover, in both its constituent sources: in the philosophy of antiquity, with its intense concern for a carefully thought out methodical programme of knowledge and research, and in the Bible, with its emphasis on the special mission and task of humanity within creation as a whole.

To describe humane research, its nature and its method, the preamble employs two particularly memorable phrases: it speaks of *assiduous* study but also of the gift of *the pearl of knowledge*. These two poles establish the magnetic field of scientific activity. In the first place and above all, science is *assiduum studium*: patient, concentrated, unremitting labour, in rigorous thinking and rigorous living. The true scientist is distinguished from the dilettante by disciplined method and from the intellectual "playboy" by his acceptance of the need for asceticism (once again, both in his thinking and in his living). It is no accident that the forerunner of the modern-style researcher is to be found in the medieval monasteries, in the ranks of those who, in a life of deliberate and intense discipline, devoted themselves unreservedly to the quest for truth and, in so doing, discovered and made accessible to others the springs of intellectual concentration. For every science, *assiduum studium is* a vital necessity.

But there is another vital necessity, too. This is indicated by the reference in the preamble to *the gift of God* and the image of *the pearl of knowledge*. The reference here to both theological and aesthetic motifs may strike us at first as rather surprising. Yet these motifs, too, are part and parcel of the self-understanding of Western science. I think here of Plato and his insistence that the discovery of truth also proceeds by way of active enthusiasm and delight in the beautiful, delight in the beauty of truth, and that it therefore includes aesthetic and even *erotic* dimensions. I am also thinking of the biblical insight that fundamental human truths, human self-discovery, are imparted to us "as in a dream", as an unearned bonus and gift. These motifs, too, have

96

their proper place in our reflections on humane research. Not, of course, as substitutes for *assiduum studium* or in competition with it, but as a reminder of its sobering and yet liberating limits. Without the life-breath of creative delight and grace, even the best-intentioned scientific enterprise can all too easily become a fruitless, cheerless and therefore unconvincing business. Our universities and scientific institutions will be well-advised to remember and accept both recommendations of the preamble: to become places of *assiduum studium* and of delight in the *margarita scientiae*. The two elements characterise academic spirituality.

Towards the good life in solidarity
The foundation bull of the University of Basle is not content to sing the praises of scientific research; it also raises and answers the question *of the aim and purpose of science and knowledge.* Two points here seem to me especially relevant for our purpose. The splendid image of *the pearl of knowledge* is followed immediately, almost in the same breath as it were, by the qualifying clause (omitted in the wall inscription): *quae bene beateque vivendi viam prebet.* This *margarita scientiae* "points the way to the good and happy life". Human knowledge, in other words, is not an end in itself, a static self-contained goal; it is not a *scientia pro scientia,* unconnected with other fundamental aspects of human life. Quite the contrary: it is connected with the whole of life wherein it has its special yet at the same time ministerial role. This role is the service of life, indeed, the service of the *good and happy* life. It is commended only as *humane* knowledge, knowledge which is of benefit to humanity.

This impressive phrase *"bene beateque vivere"* confronts the university and Western science with the fundamental *ethical* question of the purpose and aims of scientific research and also, concretely, of its consequences and acceptance of responsibility for them. Reviewing the triumphal march of science it is hard to avoid the impression that this important ethical aspect of its problems has been neglected and often suppressed. Scientific research has for centuries been regarded as an enterprise "beyond good and evil". In some respects, there were understandable grounds for this: the desire, for example, to safeguard against the imposition of moralistic and even ideological "leading strings" on scientific work. Against this, it was argued that the scientist's only ethic was the obligation to use impeccable methods. What is demanded of the researcher is thorough research. He is not to let himself be bothered or side-tracked by the consideration of possible consequences. The question of *"bene beateque vivere"* was deliberately left out of account.

Among scientists with a sense of responsibility, this question is coming right into the forefront of attention today. In the first place, it was raised among the nuclear physicists, and there in a particularly dramatic way. The "Oppenheimer case" has rightly acquired the character of an example, along with the American physicist's confession that "for the first time, the scientist has known sin". Researchers in other fields, too, biologists, medical doctors, chemists and others, are taking a lively interest in ethical questions today - in Basle, for example. There is a growing consensus that the scientist has an obligation to ask not only the technical question as to whether something *can* be done but also the ethical and political question as whether it *ought* to be done. Science's capacity to do something is not ethically neutral. Science is power and power confronts us with questions concerning our ethical and political responsibility for its use. The foundation charter is right. Only when it aims at a "good and happy life" does knowledge shine with the pristine lustre of a pearl; i.e. only as research for the benefit of humanity.

Another phrase in the preamble points in the same direction. The sign and the goal of the knowledge we are to seek is that it *"uplifts to the very heights those born in the humblest estate"*. The primary reference here, of course, is to the intellectual rank of scientists, the special dignity which "clearly distinguishes the knowledgeable person from the ignorant". At the same time, however, the intellectual rank also has a social dimension which seems to me worth noting. Did not the status conferred by knowledge sometimes make it possible even in the Middle Ages for scholars to cross the barriers of a social order determined by birth? I would like to pick this up and, following the inherent dynamic of this motif, deliberately extend its application by a further relevant emphasis. Scientific research, if it is to benefit humanity, must be directed especially to *those born in the humblest estate.*

In every age, of course, advanced research is primarily the work of the intellectual elite (the "*periti*" and "*sublimes*"); this certainly does not mean, however, that it need remain a purely elitist concern, an alliance of interest between profit and privilege. That this temptation exists can hardly be denied. But to succumb to it would be a betrayal of the spirit of Western science as reflected in our preamble. Scientific research which is of benefit to humanity owes an obligation to the *res publica*, to the community, which means, in particular, an obligation to those who are worst off in any given situation. At the end of the 20th century, this focus on the *res publica* cannot halt at the city boundaries or at the frontiers of one country but must take into account the interests of the underprivileged throughout the world; it must be directed to the *populorum progressio,* the "development of the peoples", to use the phrase made famous by one of Pius II's successors in our own day.

I realise, of course, that the direction hitherto taken by Western science has never yet matched anything like adequately these broad objectives of humane scientific research, despite all our democratic and social achievements. A great deal is still to be done in both science and politics. Does that mean that our preamble's standpoint is merely unrealistic utopianism? I would hope not. Initial steps have been taken suggesting a change in outlook in the direction indicated. I am thinking, for example, of renewed efforts to make access to our universities easier for the disabled - not only access in the broader sense but also in the physical sense (by at last undertaking the structural alterations required to ensure that the disabled are not confronted with almost insuperable obstacles at every step and turn). I am also thinking of the (certainly still too slowly) growing recognition that our centres of learning also have obligations to the developing countries and must learn to fulfil them more effectively. Following the direction indicated in our preamble, it is in this respect in particular that the dynamic inherent in the term *Uni-*

versitas is to be developed in a spirit of solidarity.

The perspective of the 'nevertheless'

There is a persistent note of *confidence and hope* in the words of the foundation charter of the University of Basle. The founder is deeply persuaded of the good sense of his foundation. The overall horizon of meaning in which he sees this university leaves him no room for doubt on this score. He is convinced that the human passion for truth and knowledge is no vain clutching at thin air. Assiduous study attains the goal; the way to the good and happy life is open; even those born in the humblest estate can achieve the heights.

Such hopeful tones are only too familiar to us in the history of modern science. From the Renaissance right down to the 19th century via humanism and the Enlightenment this entire era was undoubtedly marked by an almost uninterrupted mood of optimism and belief in progress. The sun is dawning on the human race and we are on the way, finally and irresistibly, to the good and happy life. Our science and knowledge provide the keys of both heaven and earth.

Today, however, in the face of the ambivalence of the consequences of scientific progress, we have largely lost this utter confidence of earlier times. To many it now seems incredible and even suspect. Does that pervasive note of confidence, then, still have anything at all to say to us? I believe it has, but on one condition, namely, that we listen very carefully to what the preamble actually says and do not immediately equate it with the optimistic views of subsequent modernism. The confidence reflected in the preamble is not of a fanatical and unqualified kind but rather a sober, realistic and conditional confidence.

We note that the first and key adjective used in the preamble to define humanity is *mortalis*. Humanity is mortal, subject to death. Knowledge of the boundary established for us as human beings by death and by the penchant for destruction cooperating with it in the background is assumed by the author of the preamble; it is an integral part of his view of human life. *Memento mori* (Remember death!) is the watchword of the Middle Ages - in life as in science. The medievals were far more sober and realistic than we moderns in this respect. For it is surely undeniable that the reality of death and of the destructive potential universally present in us human beings has come to be repeatedly suppressed and explained away in the course of modern times. Only by this suppression did the dream of irresistible progress and the delusion of omnicompetence become possible. The foundation charter of our university indulges in no such dream, succumbs to no such delusion. Its promise is held out to *mortal* humanity.

But that is precisely the point: the promise is for us mortals. "In this fallible life" *(in hac labili vita)*, not everything is in vain. According to the preamble, our mortal life is embedded in a broad, supportive horizon of meaning. The basis underlying and supporting this horizon is *God*. The word "God" occurs twice in the preamble: at the beginning, where the foundation of the university, the human capacity for knowledge, and knowledge itself, are understood as *ex dono Dei,* as God's good gift; and at the end, where humanity is finally defined in terms of "likeness to God" *(Deo similis)*. In other words, scientific research in general and the universities in particular are not fortuitous, arbitrary creations. They have in God's sight a mission and a promise. This confirms the responsibility of scientists, confirms the summons to engage in scientific research which seeks to benefit humanity. But it also confirms and substantiates confidence and a sober hope in respect of this enterprise.

This theological perspective can also throw light, perhaps, on the daily life of students and scientists, for their learning and searching. Every science has its times of success but also its times of failure. Every research institute echoes occasionally to the joyful cry of *"eureka!"* but sighs of dejection and scepticism are also heard, as well as the question, "What's the point of it all?" How frequently has the situation of the scientist - and that of modern man generally - been likened to and interpreted in terms of the situation of the mythical Sisyphus! I am thinking, for example, of Albert Camus' penetrating interpretation of *la condition humaine.* Is this not, in fact, the situation of the scientist (and of all of us, students and teachers) every single day of our lives: every day having to push or drag the stone a little further up the hill of knowledge - or even the mountain of death - only in the end to find, time and again, that the stone rolls backward down the hill again? To be honest, realistic, cherishing no illusions - is this not a parable of our human condition?

I would not deny or even minimise in the slightest that this sisyphean view does indeed respect human dignity. Yet our preamble discloses another way, a "third way" between optimism and pessimism. As we have seen, the preamble recognises, even expressly refers to, the infirmity and "fallibility" of human life. By naming the name of God, however, it introduces the liberating dimension of a horizon of meaning which encompasses every success and failure: it introduces the *perspective of the "nevertheless"*. Expressed pictorially, over against the stone of Sisyphus it sets the stone of the Easter story, the stone which was rolled away from the tomb of Jesus. *Ex dono Dei,* the power of death is not an ultimate power.

As is impressively clear in the foundation charter of our university, the way taken by our culture and its scientific research has been deeply marked by this hope despite all deviations to one side or the other, whether optimistic or pessimistic. This perspective, it seems to me, is important both for our personal life and for our life in the university and society. Far from removing us to a distance from Sisyphus, it makes us, on the contrary, his kinsfolk and colleagues. We are not spared the backward-rolling stones. Both in science and in life stones are more common than pearls. Yet this perspective also makes us Sisyphus' kinsfolk *ex dono Dei,* i.e. with hope before us. It is the paramount task of theology within the university to recall this perspective.

What this might mean in practice for our daily life of research may be expressed as follows: the reference to God takes the pressure off us and at the same time encourages us. It *takes the pressure off us:* we are *not* omnicompetent "fixers", the lords of life and death. We are not called upon to assume the part of Atlases who must bear the destiny of humanity in life and in death on their shoulders. There is the "Lamb of God who takes away the sin of the world" (John 1:29). Once we know this, not the responsibility, but the pressure is taken off us. Moreover, it *encourages us: ex dono Dei* we are no longer fighting a losing battle. Our learning, our science, our life - all these are under the abiding "promise of the nevertheless". It is not pointless and futile for us, either as human beings or as scientists in our faculties and institutions, to push or drag our small or huge stones a few paces up the steep hill in our scientific research for the benefit of humanity.

NOTES

Chapter 1
1491-1500: *DECENNIUM MIRABILE* OR *ZWISCHEN DEN ZEITEN?*, Jaroslav Pelikan

1 Herbert Butterfield, *The Whig Interpretation of History* (London, 1931), p 43.
2 Johann Wolfgang von Goethe, *Faust*, lines 570-3; translation my own.
3 Karl Barth, *Die protestantische Theologie im 19. Jahrhundert: Ihre Vorgeschichte und ihre Geschichte* (Zurich, 1947), p 5.
4 Jaroslav Pelikan, *Reformation of Church and Dogma (1300-1700)* (Chicago, 1984), pp 10-126: 'Doctrinal Pluralism in the Later Middle Ages' and 'One, Holy, Catholic, andApostolic?'
5 In this enterprise I have been aided by Bernard Grun, *The Timetables of History* (New York, 1982), and Karl Heussi, *Zeittafeln zur Kirchengeschichte* (2d ed., Tübingen, 1919).
6 Leslie J Macfarlane, *William Elphinstone and The Kingdom of Scotland 1431-1514: The Struggle for Order* (Aberdeen, 1985), pp 319-20. Hereafter I shall refer to this basic work simply as 'Macfarlane' with the number of the page.
7 John W O'Malley, *The First Jesuits* (Cambridge, Massachusetts, 1993), p 226; the entire section subtitled 'The Faith in Education', pp 208-15, is an exposition of the philosophy underlying this 'educational style'.
8 Macfarlane, p 390.
9 M-D Chenu, *La théologie au douzième siècle* (2d ed., Paris, 1966), pp 210-20.
10 Beryl Smalley, *The Study of the Bible in the Middle Ages* (Notre Dame, 1964), p 331.
11 Charles Augustus Briggs, *History of the Study of Theology* (2 vols; New York, 1916), 2:98.
12 '*Musas elegantiores ... restituit ac hebraicam simul et grecam linguam ab interitu reduxit*': quoted in Heiko Augustinus Oberman, *Werden und Wertung der Reformation: Vom*

Wegestreit zum Glaubenskampf (Tübingen, 1977), p 22, n 17.

13 Macfarlane, p 368.

14 Paul Oskar Kristeller, *Renaissance Thought: The Classic, Scholastic, and Humanistic Strains* (New York, 1961), p 79.

15 Macfarlane, pp 300-1.

16 Macfarlane, p 382, and p 401, n 242, citing the unpublished work of R K French, *The establishment of medical teaching in the Universities of Aberdeen from 1495-1860.*

17 Etienne Gilson, *L'esprit de la philosophie médiévale* (2d ed., Paris, 1944), p 377.

18 Macfarlane, pp 304-5, 323.

19 See PA Duhamel, 'The Oxford lectures of John Colet', *Journal of the History of Ideas,* XIV (1953), pp 493-510.

20 Macfarlane, p 389.

21 Macfarlane, p 323, p 374.

22 F Stegmaller, *Repertorium commentariorum in Sententias Petri Lombardi* (2 vols; Warzburg, 1947).

23 WD Simpson (ed.), *Quatercentenary of the death of Hector Boece, first Principal of the University of Aberdeen* (Aberdeen 1937).

24 Macfarlane, p 323, p 390.

25 Robert J Getty, 'Alexander Souter 1873-1949', *Proceedings of the British Academy,* XXXVIII (1952), pp 255-68.

26 Macfarlane, pp 365-6, p 390.

27 Jaroslav Pelikan, *Christianity and Classical Culture: The Metamorphosis of Natural Theology in the Christian Encounter with Hellenism* (New Haven, 1993), p 3.

28 Adolf von Harnack, *Das Wesen des Christentums* (4th ed; Leipzig, 1901), p 126.

Chapter 2
THE PLACE OF THEOLOGY IN THE FOUNDATION OF THE UNIVERSITY, G Patrick Edwards

(L. = Latin text; E. = English translation)

1   For the general background, H Rashdall, *The Universities of Europe in the Middle Ages*, 2nd ed. by FM Powicke and AB Emden, (Oxford, 1936), esp. vol. 1, pp xxiv, 1-24.
2   LJ Macfarlane, *William Elphinstone and the Kingdom of Scotland, 1431-1514* (Aberdeen, 1985), ch 7, esp. pp 290-6 on Elphinstone's visit to Rome; and 372-82 on theology and canon law at King's.
3   Gordon Donaldson (tr.), "The Foundation Charters" in FC Eeles, *King's College Chapel, Aberdeen* (A.U. Studies no. 136, Edinburgh, 1956), pp 136-265: L. and E. (followed here with some minor changes); the passages cited are from pp 138-43 (1495); 154-9, 162-9 and 174-81 (1505); 198-201 (1531).
4   Hector Boece, *Murthlacensium et Aberdonensium Episcoporum Vitae*, J Moir (ed. and tr.), (New Spalding Club, Aberdeen, 1894), pp 89f: L. and E.
5   JG Riddell, "Divinity", in *Fortuna Domus*, Lectures in commemoration of the fifth centenary of the foundation of the University of Glasgow, (Glasgow, 1952), p 2; but see also J Durkan and J Kirk, *The University of Glasgow 1451-1577* (Glasgow, 1977), pp 109-26.
6   Boece, op. cit. (n 4), pp 91-3; PJ Anderson, *Aberdeen Friars: Red, Black, White, Grey* (A.U. Studies no. 40, Aberdeen, 1909), pp 68-72; Durkan and Kirk, op. cit. (n 5), pp 114f, 171f.
7   PS and HM Allen (eds.), *Opus Epistolarum D. Erasmi* vol. 7 (1928), p 399, Ep. 1996: L.
8   Mgr JC Barry (ed. and tr.), *William Hay's Lectures on Marriage* (Stair Society Publications no. 24, Edinburgh, 1967): L. and E.
9   For the Visitation of 1549: C Innes (ed.), *Fasti Aberdonenses 1494-1854* (Spalding Club, Aberdeen, 1854) pp 259-72: L.

10 PJ Anderson (ed.), *Officers and Graduates of University and King's College Aberdeen* (New Spalding Club, Aberdeen, 1893), pp 324-48: L.; David Stevenson, *King's College, Aberdeen, 1560-1641: From Protestant Reformation to Covenanting Revolution* (Quincentennial Studies series, Aberdeen, 1990): with E., pp 149-66.

11 GD Henderson (Professor of Church History, 1924-57), *The Founding of Marischal College Aberdeen* (A.U. Studies no. 123, Aberdeen, 1947), esp. pp 44-72 on "The Religious Interest". For the Earl Marischal's foundation charter: PJ Anderson (ed.), *Fasti Academiae Mariscallanae Aberdonensis*, vol. 1 (New Spalding Club, Aberdeen, 1899), pp 39-77: L. and E.; esp. p 47 for the students' Sunday reading, the wording on which is virtually identical with that of King's New Foundation (cf n. 10).

Chapter 3
'THE FEAR OF THE LORD IS THE BEGINNING OF WISDOM': THE BIBLICAL WARRANT FOR A UNIVERSITY AND MUCH ELSE BESIDES, William Johnstone

1 This essay started off life as a sermon on Daniel 1 preached at the Divinity Opening Service, King's College Chapel, Aberdeen, 9 October 1992; it now bears a somewhat distant relation to its origins.

2 Examples of the use of the text can be found from King James VI at the beginning of *Basilicon Doron* (1602 ed., p 2) to a child's scribble in the first volume of the Ellon Kirk Session minutes, IJ Simpson, *Education in Aberdeenshire before 1872* (University of London Press, London, 1947), p 23.

3 It is planned that a major series on Smith - a volume of essays read at a congress held in Aberdeen in April 1994 to mark the centenary of his death; the Gifford Lectures on Smith by John W Rogerson in April and May, 1994; and an edition of Smith's hitherto unpublished *Second and Third Series of Burnett Lectures on the Religion of the Semites* by

John Day - will all be published in 1995 by Sheffield Academic Press.

4 JS Black, G Chrystal, *Lectures and Essays of William Robertson Smith* (A&C Black, London, 1912), p 135.

5 Biographical sketch of Smith by his father, William Pirie Smith (dated from internal evidence to about 1883), which is preserved among the MSS in the possession of Christ's College, Aberdeen, p 35.

6 On the north wall immediately east of the pulpit. A fund standing now (1994) at over £37,000 was endowed by the late Dr William Lillie to replace this calamitous window, devoid of artistic merit except perhaps for the totally stylised figures by Sir Edward Burne Jones, of four "prophets" (including Daniel! - rightly excoriated by Dr Alexander Webster at the time as a "solecism" doing no honour to Smith's biblical scholarship).

7 From the report in the Aberdeen *Daily Free Press*, 1 September 1897.

8 The words are from TM Lindsay's obituary article on Smith, 'Pioneer and Martyr of the Higher Criticism: Professor William Robertson Smith', *The Review of the Churches*, vol. 6, no. 31, April 14, 1894, p 42.

9 Smith's own vocabulary in *The Religion of the Semites*.

10 'On the question of prophecy in the Critical Schools of the Continent', first published in April 1870 (as part of his - successful - candidacy for the Chair of Hebrew in the Free Church College, Aberdeen), now in *Lectures and Essays*, pp 164f.

11 "Before he was twelve years old, he had several attacks of illness so severe that once and again his life was despaired of, but also in the course of these years we had the consolation of learning that a work of grace was wrought upon him and in such a form that he was at length delivered from the fear of death and made partaker of a hope full of immortality. That the change ... was real, we had many satisfactory evidences - not the less satisfactory that there was no parade of piety, no sanctimoniousness, but a cheerful performance of daily duty, truthfulness in word and deed, and a conscien-

tiousness which we could not help thinking was sometimes almost morbid" (Pirie Smith, MS Biography, p 2, quoted for the most part in JS Black, G Chrystal, *Life of William Robertson Smith* (A&C Black, London, 1912), p 12).

12 "[I]n our country the critical method seems most to call for exposition, especially in view of the unscrupulous pertinacity with which the enemies of Christianity in England are accustomed to claim every critic as a witness on their side" (*Lectures and Essays*, p 164).

13 *Lectures and Essays*, p 120.

14 "The knowledge given in revelation is not the knowledge of facts but the knowledge of a Person. What God reveals is simply HIMSELF" (Smith's caps.), ibid., p 123.

15 The term is used in *The Scotsman* obituary of Smith (2 April 1894): "Many fought on his side who did not hold his views ... They believed the [critical] questions were not settled by the Confession, and they were resolved that the Confession should not be extruded by a judicial decision."

16 As he is about extension of ecclesiastical authority: he would have had no truck with the Board of Nomination to Theological Chairs. In a letter to *The Scotsman*, 31 March 1883, Smith argued that theology could only be appropriately carried out in the Scottish universities if it were freed from attachment to the Established Church. "... [T]here are ... a good many people ... who hold that the Theological Faculties ... might be something more, and were something more in the original conception of our Universities. Theology found a place in the University system because it was held to be a science; nay, the highest of all sciences, useful ... as part of the circle of higher culture ... When it is said that nobody wants scientific theology [but denominational], this really means ... that General Assemblies ... do not wish candidates for the ministry to attend the lectures of men who are free to teach in matters of religion whatever they believe to be true and capable of scientific proof."

17 *Answer*, pp 24-25.

18 Cf *Free Church of Scotland Monthly* shortly after his death: "it may be proper to correct some of the impressions which

are at present abroad ... One is that he was deposed. That is not true. Another is that his teaching was declared to be 'heretical'. That, too, is not the case. All that occurred was this, that he was dismissed from his chair because it was held that he had so far lost the confidence of the church as to be unable any longer to teach with general acceptance."

19 "The Arabs are immensely impressed by the kind of power embodied in our industries and trade, by the power of English [sic!] knowledge to control the forces of nature for the service of man ... The idea is certainly gaining ground that England [sic!] is the country whose protectorate would be most acceptable and most fruitful in good results" ('A Journey in the Hejaz. I', *Lectures and Essays*, pp 493, 495 [article written from Jeddah, 11 January and first published in *The Scotsman*, 3 March, 1880]). I suppose the United Nations is the analogue today.

20 E.g., his assumptions of survivals of early practice in his *Religion of the Semites*.

21 As EW Heaton wittily put it long ago, *Solomon's New Men: The Emergence of ancient Israel as a national state* (Thames & Hudson, London, 1974), p 123.

22 Cf Smith: "[N]o knowledge of phenomena will save man - it is personal acquaintance with God that is required. And so soon as this is given all other knowledge receives its proper significance", *Lectures and Essays*, p 125.

Chapter 4
THE FEAR OF THE LORD - THEN AND NOW, Howard Marshall

1 I am told that the secret of Hebrew poetry is that it consists of couplets of the form "x, and, what is more, y", where a statement is followed by a second statement which takes the matter a bit further by saying it differently, or stating the converse, or whatever.

2 Cf also Prov. 15:33: "The fear of the LORD is instruction in wisdom, and humility goes before honour."

3   The topic may be pursued further in RE Clements, *Wisdom in Theology* (Paternoster Press, Carlisle, 1992).

4   For useful surveys see FW Burnett, "Wisdom", in JB Green (et al.), *Dictionary of Jesus and the Gospels* (IVP, Leicester, 1992), pp 873-7; EJ Schnabel, "Wisdom", in GF Hawthorne (et al.), *Dictionary of Paul and his Letters* (IVP, Leicester, 1993), pp 967-73.

5   The key passages are Matt. 11:19, 28-30; 12:42; 23:34, 37; Luke 7:35; 11:31, 49.

6   The use of the verb *sebomai* is much more common in this context, Acts 13:43, 50; 16:14; 17:4, 17; 18:7). The view that these phrases refer to Gentiles who worshipped God but had not become full proselytes has been strongly contested, but the balance of opinion is in favour of the traditional understanding.

7   PH Towner, *The Goal of our Instruction* (JSOT Press, Sheffield, 1989), pp 147-52.

Chapter 5
THE WISDOM OF GOD AND THE WISDOM OF THE WORLD : THEOLOGY AND THE UNIVERSITY, Brian S Rosner

1   In Carl Andresen and Günter Klein (eds.), *Theologia Crucis - Signum Crucis: Festschrift für Erich Dinkler zum 70 Geburtstag,* (JCB Mohr, Tübingen, 1979), pp 57-71; p 59.

2   Cf 1 John 4:5: "they [unbelievers] are of the world, therefore what they say is of the world".

Chapter 6
STUDY ROOTED IN DEVOTION - THE ABERDEEN THEOLOGICAL TRADITION, Ian Bradley

1   Quoted in AM Allchin, *The Dynamic of Tradition* (Darton, Longman and Todd, London, 1981), p 67.

2 DB Calhoun, entry on Scougal in *Dictionary of Scottish Church History and Theology* (T & T Clark, Edinburgh, 1993), p 762.
3 Ibid.
4 Quoted in M. Reith, *Beyond the Mountains* (SPCK, London, 1979), p 69.
5 Ibid, p 70.
6 GD Henderson, *Mystics of the North East* (3rd Spalding Club, Aberdeen, 1934). This is one of the few published works to be devoted to an aspect of the Aberdeen spiritual tradition. Another, the only full published study of the Aberdeen Doctors, is D Macmillan, *The Aberdeen Doctors* (Hodder & Stoughton, London, 1909).

Chapter 7
THOMAS REID ON THE OBJECTIVITY OF MORALS, David Fergusson

1 A lecture delivered at London University reproduced in the *Church Times*, 3 June 1994, p 10.
2 Ibid.
3 JL Mackie, *Ethics: Inventing Right and Wrong* (Penguin, Harmondsworth, 1977).
4 The principal source of biographical information on Reid is the excellent biography by A Campbell Fraser, *Thomas Reid* (Oliphant, Anderson and Ferrier, Edinburgh, 1898).
5 Ibid., p 52.
6 Ibid., p 59.
7 'Of First Principles in General', *Essays on the Intellectual Powers of Man* (John Bell, Edinburgh, 1785), pp 555-75.
8 'The First Principles of Contingent Truths', ibid., pp 575-604.
9 This religious contrast between Hume and Reid is drawn by Alexander Broadie, *The Tradition of Scottish Philosophy* (Polygon, Edinburgh, 1990), pp 105-18.
10 *Thomas Reid* (Routledge, London, 1989), p 20.

11 *Essays on the Active Powers* (John Bell, Edinburgh, 1788), p 231.

12 Ibid., p 228.

13 Ibid., p 230.

14 Ibid., p 251. It is on the basis of this theory of an innate moral sense that Reid in Essay V contests Hume's view that justice is an artificial virtue framed for our social convenience.

15 Ibid., p 264.

16 Ibid., p 255. It must be admitted, however, that Reid's stress on the universal consent to the principles of common sense irrespective of education in the *Essays on the Intellectual Powers* stands in some tension with the emphasis upon the significance of training in the *Essays on the Active Powers.*

17 Ibid., pp 371ff.

18 For a discussion of the influence of Reid's philosophy see Sydney E Ahlstrom, 'The Scottish Philosophy and American Philosophy', *Church History*, 24 (1955), pp 257-72; Paul Helm, 'Thomas Reid, Common Sense and Calvinism', *Rationality in the Calvinian Tradition,* Hendrik Hart, Johan Van Der Hoeven, & Nicholas Wolterstorff (eds.), (University Press of America, Lanham MD, 1983), pp 71-89.

19 In a speech delivered at the presentation of the Templeton Prize 1994 as reported in *Church Times*, 13 May 1994, p 9.

20 *Whose Justice? Which Rationality?* (Duckworth, London, 1988), pp 324-5.

21 *Essays on the Active Powers*, op. cit., p 381.

22 Ibid., p 283.

23 Cf John Hick, 'The Universality of the Golden Rule', *Ethics, Religion and the Good Society*, Joseph Runzo (ed.), (Westminster/John Knox Press, Louisville, 1992), pp 155-66.

24 Jeffrey Stout, *Ethics After Babel* (Clarke, Cambridge, 1988), p 214.

Chapter 9
MARRYING WISDOM AND WITNESS. A NEW FOUN-
DATION FOR PRACTICAL THEOLOGY, William Forbes
Storrar

The author gratefully acknowledges the assistance of Morton
Gauld who translated the extracts from *Ecclesiastes* (ASD,
V-4).
1 *Scottish Journal of Theology,* vol. 33, p 2.
2 See John Durkan, 'Early Humanism and King's College,
   Aberdeen', *Aberdeen University Review* XLVIII (1979-80),
   pp 259-79; and Leslie Macfarlane, *William Elphinstone and
   the Kingdom of Scotland 1431-1514* (Aberdeen University
   Press, Aberdeen, 1985).
3 Wolfhart Pannenberg, *Theology and the Philosophy of Science* (Darton, Longman & Todd, London, 1976), pp 438-9.
4 Leon-Ernest Halkin, *Erasmus: A Critical Biography*
   (Blackwell, Oxford, 1993), p 13.
5 *Erasmi Opera Omnia* [ASD] (Amsterdam: Elsevier, 1991),
   V-4, pp146-7, 309-18.
6 Olav Myklebust, *The Study of Missions in Theological Education* (Egede Institute, Oslo, 1955) vol. 1, p 37.
7 See David S Cairns, *The Faith That Rebels* (SCM, London,
   1928); and his contributions to *The International Review of
   Missions.* As author of the report on 'The Missionary Message in Relation to Non-Christian Religions' at the World
   Missionary Conference, Edinburgh 1910, Cairns was an advocate of "thorough teaching in Comparative Religions" in
   all theological colleges, and the establishment of lectureships
   on special religions.
8 ASD, V-4, 518-520.
9 *Archive für Reformationsgeschichte*, 65, p106.
10 ASD, V-4, 302-585.
11 Luis Rivera, *A Violent Evangelism: The Political and Religious Conquest of the Americas* (Westminster/John Knox
   Press, Louisville, 1992), p 249.
12 Macfarlane, p 448.

Chapter 10
ABERDEEN UNIVERSITY AND THE STUDY OF RELIGIONS, James Thrower

1   For the attitude of the Fathers of the Christian Church to pagan religions cf Pinard de la Boulaye, *L'Étude comparée des religions*, vol. 1, p 55. It is interesting to note, however, that, some half a century before Marx's work on the social origins of religion, the Professor of Natural History at Marischal College, Aberdeen, James Hay Beattie, was offering an explanation of the religions of Classical Antiquity in social and economic terms. Cf Paul B Wood, *The Aberdeen Enlightenment: The Arts Curriculum in the Eighteenth Century* (AUP, Aberdeen, 1993), p 148.

2   Those to whom this contribution is not well known should consult Anand Chitnis, *The Scottish Enlightenment* (Croom Helm, London, 1976) and Jennifer J Carter and Joan H Pittock (eds.), *Aberdeen and the Enlightenment* (AUP, Aberdeen, 1987).

3   Cf Paul Wood on the Arts curriculum at Aberdeen in the eighteenth century in his book referred to in footnote 1 above.

4   Cf Peter Rivière, 'JF McLennan and William Robertson Smith: The Aberdeen Roots of British Social Anthropology', See note 3 of W Johnstone's article in this volume.

5   Eric Sharpe, *Comparative Religion*: A *History* (Duckworth, London, 1975), p 77.

6   Cf AJ Arberry's essay on Nicholson in his *Oriental Essays: Portraits of Seven Scholars* (Allen and Unwin, London, 1960), pp 197-232.

7   W Robertson Smith, *Kinship and Marriage in Early Arabia* (CUP, Cambridge, 1885), p 223.

8   See note 3 of W. Johnstone's article in this volume.

9   Cf for example the opening words, written in 1983, of WA Graham's article 'Islam in the Mirror of Ritual' in RG Hovannisian and S Vyronis (eds.) *Islam's Understanding of Itself* (Udena Publications, Malibu, CA, 1983), that "any study of religious ritual, and particularly ritual in Islam must begin with the work of W Robertson Smith".

10 *The Times*, 19 July 1929.
11 For an assessment of Farquhar's contribution to missionary thought cf Eric J Sharpe, *Not to Destroy But to Fulfil* (Gleerup, Uppsala, 1965).
12 Riddoch had been senior classics master at Robert Gordon's College, Aberdeen, and Rector of Mackie Academy, Stonehaven. Cf *Who's Who*, 1942. I have, unfortunately, been unable to ascertain from where Riddoch acquired his interest in the Comparative Study of Religions.
13 Court Minutes, 11 February 1947. I must express my thanks to Mr David Jones of the University Registry for providing me with references to Court and Senatus minutes relating to the Riddoch bequest.
14 Among visitors to the department in its early years were Desmund Tutu, James Irvine (a leading authority on Maori Religion), Carl Starkloff (an authority on Native American Religion), and Albert Moore, author of the innovative study, *Iconography in World Religions* (1975), written whilst he was in Aberdeen.
15 For a fuller account of the history of the Department of Religious Studies in Aberdeen cf Andrew F Walls' contribution 'Scotland' to the section on 'Religious Studies in the Universities' in Ursula King (ed.), *Turning Points in Religious Studies* (T & T Clark, Edinburgh, 1990).
16 Wilfred Cantwell Smith, *Towards a World Theology* (Westminster Press, Philadelphia 1981).